Super Omnia Bonae Voluntatis

God's Good Servant
and the King's

A Hero Is Chosen Series
Hero Stories of the Saints

Book One

Reflections of an Uncommon Monk
Toward a Theology of Hero-Sainthood

Book Two

Mission of the Maiden
The Hero Story of Joan of Arc

Book Three

God's Good Servant and the King's
The Hero Story of Thomas More

Book Four

King of Kings
The Hero Story of Jesus of Nazareth

Book Five

Friar, Priest, and Martyr
The Hero Story of Maximilian Kolbe

Book Six

A Vocation Story Never Told
A Hero Story of Future Saints

Book Seven

Hero Bible Verses
Meditations of a Saint

God's Good Servant and the King's

The Hero Story of Thomas More

Brother Emmanuel Labrise, O.S.B.

A Hero Is Chosen

Book Three

Saint Joseph Books

Table of Contents

Introduction to the Series

Reflections of an Uncommon Monk is the first book in the A Hero Is Chosen series and serves as its spiritual and moral foundation. Beginning with the second book, *Mission of the Maiden,* all of the stories build on the topics and themes introduced in *Reflections of an Uncommon Monk.* The primary aim of this series is to transmit Christian spiritual principles and to teach moral virtue in the context of a hero-saint story.

A note here should be made on the central concept and predominant themes in each book beginning with *Mission of the Maiden.* Each story, whether historical or fictional, tells the tale of one or more hero-saints called by God to a particular vocation and chosen by him to fulfill a personal mission. Historical context is crucial. A large portion of each book is dedicated to placing the protagonist within his or her historical setting in which he or she is offered an opportunity to perform a task or set of tasks, and endure an event or set of events, that qualifies him or her for hero-sainthood. In all cases except Remmy Kimm, who appears in the fiction tale, *A Vocation Story Never Told,* this occurs during the latter part of their lives, sometimes lasting years or as little as one day.

The timeframe is less important than the hero-event or hero-moment itself. One may become a hero-saint through a single heroic act at the end of one's life or through a lifetime of unselfish service. Dom Tom Mo, the other protagonist in *A Vocation Story Never Told*, was called to sacrifice his life for the passengers aboard his spacecraft within the span of a few hours. Remmy Kimm, on the other hand, was called to years of missionary service and to survive a near-death experience. Both are martyrs, one red (blood, death) and the other white (selfless service to others).

Also less important than the hero-event and hero-moment is the station in life one occupies when he or she is called. Joan of Arc was called out of obscurity to a public mission lasting less than a year and culminated in her being burned at the stake as a heretic. Thomas More was called out of prominence to sacrifice his high standing in English society and even his life for loyalty to the faith he had professed. Jesus of Nazareth was also called out of obscurity to a public ministry lasting about three years and ending with his crucifixion. The hero-event and hero-moment also eclipse whatever competencies or assets one possesses when called. With the possible exception of Saint Thomas More, all are underdog stories.

A second note should be made on where these books fit within the realm of literature. In my opinion, none of the books in this series, whether historical or fictional, is in the strict sense a work of biography, history, or fiction, even if they contain biographical accounts, historical content, or fiction. Much less are they hagiographies, even if they deal with the lives of canonized saints. They are instead hero-saint stories existing within the genre of nonfiction Christian literature.

Those who appreciate the work of Joseph Campbell, especially his highly influential *The Hero with a Thousand Faces*, might find something worthwhile in the pages of these books. I have not attempted to model the fictional characters on his writing, however, nor have I attempted to frame the retelling of these stories of actual historical persons based on his work on myth and mythical figures. It is more that I am attracted to the archetype and archetypical behavior of the hero-saint that lies deep within the unconscious of every human person, at least if you subscribe to Jungian theory. This archetype, like so many others, manifests itself in movies, books, art, and public performances of every age from antiquity to the popular films of today. It is the archetype of the hero-saint that serves as the psychological foundation for the stories in this series.

I thought it helpful to provide a brief lexicon of terms on which the reader may focus. I cannot provide definitions for each, however, as there is a certain fluidity of meaning depending on a person's life, but at least the mention of them will help to make the reader aware of the important aspects of each story and the subject matter and flavor of this series. The lexicon appears on the following page.

A Lexicon of Terms

1. Capstone experience
2. Death-leading-unto-eternity
3. Desert experience
4. Deus ex machina
5. Fulfillment in life
6. Hero quest
7. Hero story
8. Hero-adventure
9. Hero-event
10. Hero-moment
11. Hero-saint
12. Life journey
13. Meaning in life
14. Mission
15. Mission sequence
16. Mystery
17. Oceans of eternity
18. Personal holiness
19. Pilgrim
20. Pilgrimage
21. Purification
22. Purpose in life
23. Reward
24. Sainthood
25. Saint-in-the-making
26. Sanctification
27. Sands of time
28. Satisfaction in life
29. Tides of history
30. Value in life
31. Vocation
32. Wayfarer
33. Winds of change

Book Three

God's Good Servant
and the King's

Introduction to Book Three

As with all of the books in this series, this hero story of Thomas More strives to incorporate the spiritual themes and concepts introduced in Book One, *Reflections of an Uncommon Monk*, while placing the protagonist in his or her authentic historical context. The aim of Part One of each book is to provide a brief and realistic historical account that avoids fanciful interpretation, which is sometimes characteristic of popular Church history. Part Two of each book strives to bring into relief some of the protagonist's heroic qualities and to provide an example of Christian hero-sainthood without idealizing his or her virtues in the manner of some traditional (and dated) hagiographies. An unavoidable limitation of my approach to this series lies in its brevity, and further reading will be required in order to obtain a comprehensive understanding of the hero-saint and the complexities of his or her times.

I hope the reader will not think it too facile of me to begin this book with the famous, albeit pithy, description given of Thomas More by his contemporary fellow humanist and trusted friend—the Dutchman, Desiderius Erasmus—who summed up

More's character as a man *"omnium horarum,"* which has been translated into English as "a man for all seasons." Erasmus may have been referring to 1 Corinthians 9:22 in which Saint Paul claims to have become "all things to all people," but he was certainly referring to that pleasant mixture of More's gentle and merry nature that coalesced with his subtle and well-formed intellect. Thomas More made such good company in fact that while Henry VIII and Catherine of Aragon were still married, they insisted that he dine with them on many occasions that he might brighten their table with his agreeable company and delightful conversation.

But it is likely that by *"omnium horarum"* Erasmus was implying a greater depth of meaning than "a learned and good-natured fellow who provided agreeable dinner conversation," and it is these other connotations—especially those involving his moral character and religious commitment—that reveal the true nature of More's hero-sainthood. I have tried in these pages to bring into relief these other connotations, and toward that end I have discovered ten dimensions of More's life and character, each consisting of a combination of consonant roles which were either: (a) bequeathed to him at birth by English society or the social class into which he was born, or (b) those he was morally obliged, or felt obliged, to assume as a matter of duty, or (c) those he voluntarily accepted as a matter of conscience or religious devotion. Some of these dimensions and their corresponding roles overlap, but each deserves mention and together they serve as an object of study in its own right, at least in the context of this hero story.

The reader will remember that the whole is often greater than the sum of the parts, and this is certainly true of the unique and unrepeatable mystery that is every human life. While the use of categories is not without limitations and a system of categories can never be without flaws, categories can nevertheless serve as a useful means of organizing and understanding our world. With this in mind, I offer this list of dimensions (or roles) as a structured and tangible aid in gaining insight into Thomas More's life and hero-saint story and especially of elucidating the meaning of Erasmus' description of Thomas as a man *"omnium horarum"*:

1. Obedient son (of John More) and responsible citizen (of London, England, and Christendom)

2. Husband, father, and family man

3. Civil lawyer, civil servant, and judge

4. Statesman, diplomat, and royal servant

5. Scholar, author, and educator

6. Philosopher and Christian humanist

7. Religious ascetic and spiritual devotee

8. Suppressor of heresy and defender of the Faith

9. Servant of God and disciple of Christ

10. Martyr and hero-saint

~

Like all historical figures, Thomas More must be understood as a person of his time and not in the context of our time. We may rightly believe that he tried his best to live as perfectly as possible with respect to the roles above, even if individual authors do not always interpret his actions in the same way, or if the ways he pursued perfection do not always align with twenty-first-century standards. The imprecision of the historical record also causes some uncertainty (as is usually the case), and since much has been lost to us over the centuries, the dedicated historian must sometimes conjecture between fact and legend. Thomas More was a man of his time, but as evidenced in the many biographies written about him and in other portrayals of him in popular culture, theater, and movies, he was in some respects ahead of his time. I hope further evidence of this can be found in these pages.

~

I had the greatest of fortunes earlier in life to have lived for more than six years in England as a member of the Order of Carthusians at Saint Hugh Charterhouse in Horsham, West Sussex. Saint Hugh Priory was constructed during the late nineteenth century, but the design and architecture is according to the medieval era, and as far as I know, Saint Hugh is the last medieval-style monastery that still operates in England. Had it not been for the reign of Henry VIII or had nature or providence blessed Queen Catherine of Aragon with at least one male heir that survived his robust and headstrong father, there might still endure today English monasteries built during the Middle Ages equipped with contingents of monks chanting Gregorian melodies of former centuries rather than the picturesque ruins that dot the English landscape today. Any visitor to Saint Hugh Charterhouse—if you happen to be male and if you are fortunate enough to gain entrance into the church and chapterhouse—may study the impressive, lifelike paintings of the martyrdoms of the many Carthusians who perished during the dissolution of the English monasteries under Henry VIII. The unpleasant details are not spared, but are vividly re-presented in the hanging, drawing, and quartering of the three priors who perished while Thomas More was imprisoned in the Tower of London. More was aware of their execution and could hear the tumult from his cell. His captors had hoped that his resolve would weaken at the prospect of so torturous a death, but More did not waver, and his constitution was only strengthened by their heroic example. More told his daughter Margaret that he was inspired by their sacrifice as they wrote what must have been the final lines of their own hero-saint stories.

I do not know if those six years of my life journey spent in England bring me any closer to Thomas More, the Carthusian martyrs, John Fisher, or the other historical figures in this story, but I like to think it does. All I have left now are memories, a few mementos, and a priceless Carthusian monastic formation. For me, though, England and the Charterhouse are one point of contact with the past, of ages long gone but not entirely forgotten, of time immemorial … but not the *only* point of contact. If there is truly a spiritual exchange of gifts in the divine dispensation—

and I believe there is—then surely gifts of devotion are distributed to the faithful whether they have visited a particular place or lived in a distant land. What is most important is not physical presence, but spiritual presence.

Please remember to make use of the final few pages reserved for notes and personal reflections, and I hope you and all who read these books encounter the spiritual presence of Saint Thomas More and the other hero-saints in this series, and more importantly, the Hero-Lord they served.

Important Dates
1453 to 1935

1453   Gutenberg invents the movable type printing press

1455   Wars of the Roses (1455–1485)

1466   Birth of Desiderius Erasmus

1478   Birth of Thomas More

1483   Richard III, King of England (r. 1483–1485)
               Birth of Martin Luther

1484   Birth of Ulrich Zwingli

1485   Battle of Bosworth Field
               Henry VII, King of England (r. 1485–1509)

1491   Birth of Henry VIII

1509   Henry VIII, King of England (r. 1509–1547)
               Birth of John Calvin

1511   Luther moves to Wittenberg

1517   Luther posts his *Ninety-five Theses*

1519   Charles V, Holy Roman Emperor (r. 1519–1558)

1520   Luther threatened with excommunication

1521	Luther excommunicated
	Henry VIII awarded the title Defender of the Faith
1524	German Peasants' War (1524–1525)
1525	Luther marries Katharine von Bora
1526	William Tyndale's English translation of the New Testament printed at Worms
1527	Henry VIII begins annulment proceedings
	Sack of Rome by imperial troops under Charles V, Holy Roman Emperor
1529	Diet of Speyer (origin of the word *Protestant*)
	Thomas More becomes Lord Chancellor of England (1529–1532)
	Reformation Parliament begins in England
1532	Act of Submission of the Clergy
1533	Thomas Cranmer appointed Archbishop of Canterbury
	Act in Restraint of Appeals
	Marriage between Henry VIII and Catherine of Aragon declared null by Cranmer
	Henry VIII marries Anne Boleyn
	Anne Boleyn crowned Queen of England
1534	Act of Succession and Act of Supremacy
	Henry VIII declared Supreme Head of the Church of England by Parliament

1535	Execution of Bishop John Fisher
	Execution of Sir Thomas More
	Publication of the first complete Bible in English

1535   Execution of Bishop John Fisher
        Execution of Sir Thomas More
        Publication of the first complete Bible in English

1536   Dissolution of the Monasteries (1536–1541)

1538   Henry VIII excommunicated

1539   Publication of the Great Bible in England

1540   Execution of Thomas Cromwell

1541   Catholics and Protestants discuss reconciliation at
        Ratisbon

1545   Opening of the Council of Trent (1545–1563)

1546   Death of Martin Luther
        John Knox rises to prominence in Scotland

1547   Death of Henry VIII
        Edward VI, King of England (r. 1547–1553)
        Edward favors Protestantism
        Council of Trent moved to Bologna

1551   Second session of the Council of Trent (1551–1552)

1553   Mary I, Queen of England (r. 1553–1558)
        Mary favors Catholicism

1555   Peace of Augsburg
        Heretics against the Catholic faith burned in England
        (1555–1558)

| 1556 | Archbishop Cranmer burned at the stake in Oxford |

1558   Elizabeth I, Queen of England (r. 1558–1603)
        Elizabeth favors Protestantism

1559   John Knox returns to Scotland from exile in England
        and Switzerland

1560   Treaty of Edinburgh
        Reformed Church instituted in Scotland

1562   Beginning of the Wars of Religion in France
        Third and Final Session of the Council of Trent
        (1562–1563)

1563   Puritanism appears in England

1564   Death of John Calvin

1570   Elizabeth I excommunicated

1581   Penal laws passed against Catholics in England

1587   Execution of Mary, Queen of Scots

1603   James VI, King of Scotland, becomes James I, King
        of England (r. 1603–1625)

1935   Thomas More canonized a saint

Part One

Historical Context

Do not remember the former things,
  or consider the things of old.
I am about to do a new thing;
  now it springs forth, do you not perceive it?
I will make a way in the wilderness
  and rivers in the desert.

Isaiah 43:18–19

1

The Printing Press

There is no better place to start than from the beginning, and the beginning of history as a subject area of study is the invention of writing. Moreover, the invention of writing is the beginning of a great many other things, and it does not take a professional historian or social philosopher to appreciate the debt of gratitude we in the modern world owe to our ancestors for the invention of writing and the development of printing technology, which brought the incomparable benefit of being liberated from the distressing limitations of oral transmission.

We would do well to pause for a moment and consider that the availability of the written word today and the near universality of literacy itself are the result of a long series of events that have occurred over the millennia, and the sophisticated technologies of the modern world and our advanced education owe much to the stylus and chisel. And if the Black Death was the impetus for the slow and steady transformation of the medieval into the modern world, then the movable type printing press was its catapult. For the printing presses of Europe during the late-fifteenth century produced a proliferation of books, pamphlets, and other documents that promoted the widespread dissemination of the novel ideas of the Renaissance and Reformation. Just as gunpowder was revolutionizing warfare at this time, the printing press was revolutionizing human society, and it was no less explosive.

The origins of writing are found in Sumer in Mesopotamia and date to c. 3500–3000 BC. The early writing script used by these ancient peoples has been given the name *cuneiform* by modern scholars (L. *cuneus*, "wedge") because of the wedge-shaped impressions made by a reed stylus as it was pressed by a scribe into a wet clay tablet. Once the tablet was full of characters and the information recorded, it was left to dry in the sun and harden. The aim of this early form of writing was not to produce literature, myth, or history, nor did it utilize a sophisticated and voluminous vocabulary. Necessity being the mother of invention, writing was initially developed to satisfy the practical needs of merchants, tradesmen, and tax officials who needed a bookkeeping system that allowed them to keep track of merchandise and payments.

Thus, the earliest surviving clay tablets we have are mere mundane financial records, but as civilization advanced and walled cities and urban life began to appear in Mesopotamia and Egypt, rulers sought ways to govern larger populations more effectively. To the early pictograms (pictorial representations that signify words) of Sumerian cuneiform and Egyptian hieroglyphs were added phonograms (symbols that denote sounds), and eventually the earliest alphabets were devised by the Canaanites, Egyptians, and Minoans (e.g., Linear A and B found in the Cnossus tablets). The Phoenician cities of Tyre, Sidon, and Byblos borrowed this idea and their seafaring merchants spread it to other parts of the Mediterranean, most notably to the Greeks who added vowels to their own written symbols and produced the first complete alphabet. They also developed a simplified method of writing that made the written word more accessible to the ordinary person. This decreased the time it took to train a scribe, and instead of having to learn hundreds, and even thousands, of individual characters, a scribe needed only to learn twenty to thirty. Reading and writing became easier skills to master and literacy spread beyond an elite group of highly trained specialists. In addition, the alphabetical system was far more flexible and allowed for a greater variety of combinations that enabled authors to produce more sophisticated documents. Stories could be told, literature and history could be recorded, and scholarship was born. Rome soon adopted the alphabet, and as the legions spread Greco-Roman civilization across the Mediterranean world, Latin and Greek influenced the development of many European languages.

Writing also developed independently in China (c. 1200 BC) and Mesoamerica by the Mayans (c. 500–250 BC). Running concurrently with the invention of writing in all of these places were technological advancements in implements, inks, and writing surfaces. Clay tablets were eventually replaced by papyrus, which was first used in Egypt and later spread throughout the Mediterranean world. Papyrus was made from the pith of papyrus plants that grew in abundance along the Nile River. Parchment, a more durable but more expensive alternative to papyrus, was made by drying animal skins in the sun and then cutting them into sheets. Silk was used in the East, as was a primitive form of paper made from hemp fibers, and by 100 BC, the Chinese had invented a serviceable form of paper that could be used widely for writing. The paper industry expanded and spread west, eventually migrating to Italy in the thirteenth century and Germany in the fourteenth century.

Handwritten texts are time-consuming and laborious to produce, however, and writing technology necessarily evolved into printing technology as civilizations advanced. Woodblock printing was invented whereby a set of characters, letters, words, symbols, or illustrations was carved onto a block of wood which was then coated with ink and pressed against a sheet of paper. This technique enabled the mass production of a printed page and was first used in China during the early eighth century. There were limitations to this method, however, since one carved block face could only produce one unchangeable page, and a system of printing that used movable type (individual tiles of one character each) was needed.

Movable type printing eventually became possible as engraving techniques improved and ceramic and metal were used in place of wood, since woodblocks were difficult to produce in adequate numbers and their carvings wore down more quickly than engravings on ceramic and metal. Yet ceramic was fragile and metal surfaces required a different kind of ink than those used in woodblock printing. These difficulties impeded the widespread availability of printing presses and printed material, but by the mid-eleventh century—four hundred years before Johannes Gutenberg invented the first European printing press—the Chinese developed a system of moveable type printing that utilized ceramic tiles fixed on a metal frame. By the mid-twelfth century, books became more widely available in China, which promoted a literate and educated class of civilians. Further improvements were also made to the woodblock printing technique that allowed its continued use.

European alphabets are more conducive to movable type printing than pictogram scripts such as Sumerian cuneiform, Egyptian hieroglyphs, and Chinese characters because they are composed of a relatively small number of letters rather than thousands of individual pictograms. By 1450, Europe had its own version of a movable type printing press when Johannes Gutenberg, an inventor from Mainz, Germany, capitalized on improved metallurgical techniques and created his own individual lettered tiles using brass and lead which could be affixed to a printing plate and then wiped off and reused after a printing job was complete. This casting technique was a revolutionary step forward in itself and allowed for the production of many durable tiles. Gutenberg also mixed his own ink which could be used effectively with metal tiles, and perfected a method of flattening paper using a modified winepress. His most famous production was a Latin Vulgate known as the Gutenberg Bible, some of which were printed on paper and others on vellum (parchment).

Gutenberg's printing press was less an original invention than an ingenious combination of technological improvements, some of which he made himself. His printing technique spread rapidly during the 1450s to other cities in Germany (Strasburg, Augsburg, and Nüremberg); to Italy in the 1460s (Rome, Milan, Florence, and Naples); to France (Paris, Lyon), Flanders (Bruges in today's Belgium), and Spain (Valencia) during the 1470s; and to Portugal (Lisbon) in the 1490s. William Caxton, an Englishman, learned the printing trade in Cologne and returned from Bruges to England in 1476 to establish a printing press at Westminster Abbey where he worked until his death in 1491. Caxton is perhaps best known for his publication of Malory's *Morte d'Arthur* in 1485.

The printing press ignited a cultural revolution as significant as any in history. Books could now be mass-produced, distributed widely, and purchased at an affordable price. Literacy increased throughout Europe and knowledge that was once the exclusive domain of Europe's educated elite and aristocratic classes soon became available to the rising middle class. This had important and far-reaching consequences in the religious sphere as much as in education, since anyone could now own a Bible and interpret it for him or herself. The Gutenberg Bible was printed in Latin, but English and German versions of the Bible soon appeared and were spread abroad. The pope deemed this a threat, and indeed it was, since many of the Church's teachings and practices could not be found in Scripture. Further, the printing press facilitated the publication of pamphlets and posters as well as books. Martin Luther did not intend the widespread publication of his *Ninety-five Theses* when he posted it in 1517, but it was initially reprinted without his permission. In a word, the Reformation and its explosive consequences could not have happened without the printing press.

Klemens von Metternich (1773–1859), Chancellor and Foreign Minister of the Austrian Empire, once said of Napoleon Bonaparte (1769–1821) that he would have been successful in any age that he lived, but it was to his great advantage that he was born during the eighteenth century and reached adulthood in France at the beginning of the French Revolution. This observation refers to the convergence of *chronos* time and *kairos* time, and the same remark could be made about the movable type printing press—it would have been impactful in any age that it first appeared, but its revolutionary effects were greatly enhanced by the events that were unfolding in Europe at the time, namely:

1. The end of the Hundred Years' War in 1453 and the expulsion of English troops from France, which allowed France a period of recovery and consolidation

2. The capture of Constantinople by the Ottoman Turks, also in 1453, which put an end to the Byzantine Empire and caused Greek scholars to flee to western Europe, bringing with them ancient manuscripts that were previously unavailable to western scholars

3. The Renaissance period, particularly the progressive ideas of humanism

4. The beginning of the Age of Discovery in 1492, which supplied printers and their fascinated readership with first-hand accounts of the adventures of the early explorers and descriptions of previously unknown lands and peoples

5. The Reformation era beginning in 1517, which led to the split in Christianity and the European Wars of Religion that followed.

~

William Caxton returned to England in 1476 and printed the first book ever printed on English soil within the year, and one year before Thomas More's birth in 1478. We find here again evidence of the convergence of *chronos* and *kairos* time, and Metternich's observation may be usefully recalled: More would have been successful in any age in which he was born, but it was particularly conducive to his advancement in English society that he was born when books were beginning to be printed in England, when printing presses were proliferating on the continent, and literacy in Europe was on the rise. It is as if he were born at a *kairos* moment, as if he were *destined* to be born at a particular moment in history.[1] It is difficult in fact to imagine Thomas More

---

[1] Reading history with the eyes of faith (an appropriate way to read Christian hero stories) does not mean that we read it *eisegetically* (interpreting events by reading into it one's own ideas, beliefs, biases, and presuppositions). Rather, we strive to read and interpret history *exegetically*, that is, by trying to draw out

without reading, writing, and books, and he simply would not have been the same person without them, nor would he have had the same impact on history—even if the same could be said of Erasmus and the other influential humanists, as well as Luther and the other important reformers. Metternich's observation illustrates that meaningful events and powerful transformations occur when *kairos* time coincides with *chronos* time.

~

Although Gutenberg, Caxton, and Europe's other first printers undertook printing as a business venture and not for the purpose of promoting intellectual, religious, or political movements, they invariably fostered the democratization of knowledge, a rise in scholarship, and an intellectual egalitarianism previously unknown in history. This development brought the promise of greater enlightenment, but it also included the potential to undermine the traditional authority of the Church and state. By 1500, hundreds of printing presses were operating throughout Europe, and Alexander VI (the "Borgia Pope") felt it necessary in 1501 to threaten excommunication to those who printed books without the Church's permission.

Just as it is difficult to imagine humanists and reformers without the widespread availability of books, it is impossible to

---

of historical events what God is intending to communicate or accomplish. This approach requires that we employ skeptical empiricism and common sense that avoids fanciful interpretation as we attempt to discern God's working in history and in the lives of his saints.

imagine the Renaissance and Reformation without the printing press. Humanists utilized the printing press in the service of the Renaissance, and reformers used it in the service of the Reformation. Being in the service of someone or something, however, does not necessarily imply having less importance or power. The printing press facilitated the Renaissance and Reformation (and many other things), and if the word *revolutionary* implies being *influential*, then it is worth noting that the printing press was as revolutionary as the movements it served. Writing and printing not only record and transmit history, but they also help to shape it.

2

The Renaissance

Dating historical periods is not always a precise science. There are time periods for which it is possible to assign beginning and ending dates, but some time periods are not easily delineated. The beginning of the Norman Conquest of England, for example, can be suitably dated to the Battle of Hastings, which occurred on October 14, 1066. Just as easily dated is the end of the Byzantine Empire, which occurred on May 29, 1453, when Sultan Mehmed and the Ottoman Turks captured Constantinople. Dating the beginning and end of events like the Renaissance, however, is problematic. It is impossible in fact to determine precisely when the Renaissance began or ended since no particular person or event caused or concluded it. So how may we understand the Renaissance?

First, the word *renaissance* is a *term* that means *rebirth*. It originated with Giorgio Vasari (1511–1574) who used the word *rinascita (rebirth)* in his book *Lives of the Artists*, published in 1550, to describe the cultural and artistic revival that was occurring in Italy since the fourteenth century. *Rinascita* was translated into

French as *renaissance* (from *renaître*, revive, and *naissance*, birth), which was adopted into English during the early nineteenth century. The word *renaissance* is also used by historians to denote other time periods of cultural and intellectual revival in addition to the Renaissance we are discussing here, even if they are of lesser historical importance. These include:

a. The Carolingian renaissance of the eighth and ninth centuries

b. The Ottonian renaissance of the tenth and eleventh centuries

c. The renaissance of the twelfth century led by the school of Chartres.

Second, the Renaissance is a *time period* (c. 1350–c. 1600). While Europe was recovering during the fifteenth century from the disastrous events of the fourteenth century, the notion began to circulate among scholars that the time period between the fall of the Western Roman Empire in the fifth century (c. 476) and their contemporary times was a kind of "middle age," or a dark period in civilization ("Dark Ages"), that bridged the gap between the classical world of ancient Greece and Rome and their contemporary world. Scholars of the fifteenth and sixteenth centuries looked back for inspiration to antiquity and sought to rediscover the wisdom of ancient Greek and Roman authors. They were aided significantly when Constantinople fell to the Ottoman Turks in 1453, which precipitated the flight of Greek scholars to the West who brought with them an abundance of ancient Greek and Latin manuscripts.

To us in the modern world, the Renaissance may also be viewed as a *time period*, or a *time of transition*, that overlapped the late medieval world and the early modern period. It did not occur simultaneously and uniformly throughout Europe, however, and historians distinguish between the Southern (Italian) Renaissance (c. 1350–c. 1527[2]) and the Northern (German) Renaissance (c. 1450–c. 1600). It should also be noted that the Renaissance overlapped with the Age of Discovery which began in 1492, as well as the Reformation which began in 1517.

Third, the Renaissance was a *cultural and intellectual movement* that originated in prosperous Italian cities such as Florence (where many historians believe the Renaissance was born), Genoa, Milan, Venice, and Naples. Affluent Italian rulers and merchants accumulated great wealth from trade in the Mediterranean and used a portion of their large disposable incomes to promote the arts, sciences, and education. When most people today think of the Renaissance, their minds usually turn to Renaissance artwork, especially the paintings, sculptures, and architecture of the great masters of the High Renaissance (1480–1527), namely:

---

[2] Rome was sacked by imperial troops in 1527. This date has been conventionally cited by historians as the end of the Southern (Italian) Renaissance, but it is by no means exact.

- Leonardo da Vinci (1452–1519): *The Virgin of the Rocks* (painting, 1483–1485), *The Last Supper* (fresco, 1495–98), *Mona Lisa* (painting, 1503–1505)

- Michelangelo Buonarroti (1475–1564): *Pietà* (sculpture, 1499), *David* (sculpture, 1501–1504), *Moses* (sculpture, 1513–1515), *Dying Slave* (sculpture, 1513–1516), *Rebellious Slave* (sculpture, 1516–1519), and the ceiling fresco in the Sistine Chapel (1508–1512)

- Raphael Santi, or Sanzio (1483–1520): *The School of Athens* (fresco, 1508–1511)

- Sandro Botticelli (1445–1510): *Birth of Venus* (painting, 1482–1486) and *Pallas and the Centaur* (painting, 1482)

- Donato Bramante (1444–1514): The Tempietto at San Pietro Montorio (dome, 1502)

- Lorenzo Ghiberti (1378–1455): the bronze doors for the Baptistery of San Giovanni in Florence (1425–1452)

- Filippo Brunelleschi (1377–1446): the dome of the cathedral in Florence, Santa Maria del Fiore (1417–1436)

- Donatello (1386–1466): *Saint Mark* (sculpture, 1411–1413) and *David* (sculpture, 1430–1440)

- Hugo van der Goes (1440–1482): *The Portinari Altarpiece* (painting, 1475–1478)

- Albrecht Dürer (1471–1528), *Self-portrait at Age 28 with Fur Coat* (1500).

These timeless works of art and many others were made possible by wealthy Renaissance patrons such as the Medici, Pitti, and Strozzi families, who competed for the sponsorship of great artwork. Among the most famous of these patrons were Cosimo de' Medici (1389–1464) and his great-grandson, Lorenzo "the Magnificent" (1449–1492),[3] members of a powerful Florentine banking family. Renaissance popes such as Alexander VI (1431–1503) and Julius II (1443–1513)[4] and other high-ranking prelates also commissioned magnificent pieces of artwork to elevate the Church's reputation and for their own personal glory. These works of art were also made possible by the previous generation of artists who pioneered new artistic techniques, notably Giotto di Bondone (1266–1336), who is known as the first of the Renaissance painters and the "father of Renaissance art." His influence and that of other important proto-Renaissance painters such as Masaccio (1401–1428) was unfortunately delayed by the outbreak of the Black Death (1347–1351), which caused widespread disruption in European society.[5]

While innovations in the art world were helping to foster a *cultural renaissance* in Europe, the Renaissance also included an *intellectual movement*, the basis of which was humanism. The term *humanism*, however, did not come into use until the nineteenth century, and Renaissance scholars did not think of themselves as

---

[3] To whom Niccolo Machiavelli dedicated *The Prince*.

[4] Known to history as the "Borgia Pope" and "Warrior Pope" respectively.

[5] One of the many ways the Plague influenced medieval society was in its artwork, which became more somber and macabre.

humanists. Humanism is a vague and flexible term that has evolved and today has a variety of meanings, but what we understand as *Renaissance humanism* originated with Leonardo Bruni (1374–1444) of Florence, who first used the term *umanista* to classify the humanities as a subject area of study. Among the first to introduce humanist ideas were Petrarch (1304–1374, considered the "father of humanism"), Dante Alighieri (1265–1321), and Giovanni Boccaccio (1313–1375).

Yet even the term *Renaissance humanism* is so flexible that it is difficult to define except as a broad, general concept inclusive of numerous and sometimes conflicting ideologies. It is perhaps best understood as a philosophy of education rather than a methodology or subject area of study with its own specific content. The central idea of humanism is Protagoras' notion that "man is the measure of all things," a tenet that promoted a fundamental shift from the God-centered universe of medieval times to a human-centered worldview of the Early Modern period (which helps to explain why Renaissance humanism has been credited with fostering a spirit of individualism and promoting secular values). Humanism was not necessarily contrary to the teachings of the Church, but it created ambiguity by its rejection of scholastic obscurantism and its emphasis on humanity rather than divinity.

Just as humanism cannot be properly classified as a distinct philosophy or school of thought, humanists were never a homogeneous group of thinkers, and the content of *studia humanitatis* was always open to debate. Renaissance humanism was more a culture of learning that emphasized:

- The study of classical languages and a return to the sources (*ad fontes*) of ancient Greek and Roman texts

- Critical analysis and sound scholarship based on grammar, rhetoric (the art of persuasion, of presenting a convincing argument), and classical literature

- The rejection of medieval chivalry, Scholasticism, and for some humanists, the social and political institutions of feudalism

- The dignity of the human person and the exaltation of human nature

- The vague but appealing concept of *studia humanitatis*, a term found in the writings of Cicero (106–43 BC), which refers to the "study of humanity" or the study of what it means to be human

- And the equally flexible notion of *bonae litterae* (lit. "good letters" or "sound learning") which fosters well-developed language skills that enable one to participate effectively in public life.

Renaissance humanists sought a *rinascita,* or *rebirth,* of the knowledge and wisdom of antiquity that would help them acquire greater intellectual, moral, civic, and social virtue (L. *virtus,* strength, excellence). In looking back to the classical world for inspiration and learning, humanists promoted an educational reform movement that elevated the importance of ancient pagan literature, which was previously subordinate to the study of theology. For humanist scholars, classical literature was not merely a collection of relics left over from extinct civilizations but instead constituted a living source (L. *fons*) of knowledge whose usefulness and merit transcended time and place. Humanists advocated a "return to the sources" (*ad fontes*) and believed that the wisdom they gleaned from these ancient authors could be used in the service of Christianity and contemporary society, especially in promoting good government.

The early humanists were mostly cleric-scholars, but as books became more widely available after the invention of the printing press, humanist ideas spread north from Italy to all parts of Europe, and humanism grew in popularity among secular scholars and laymen. Although most humanists were Christian and meant no harm to the Christian faith, the Church recognized humanism as a potential threat because of its variability and wide application and its focus on pagan sources. Early reformers such as Martin Luther, John Calvin, and Ulrich Zwingli were in fact greatly influenced by humanist ideas, as were King Henry VIII and William Tyndale of England.

Humanists eventually founded public libraries and entered politics and other forms of public service including teaching, writing, and the publication of books. An increasing number of books, including Bible translations, were printed in the vernacular, which helped to standardize the common forms of languages.

The Age of Discovery, which began in 1492 with Columbus' voyage, facilitated the spread of humanist ideas to other parts of the world. The Puritans, for example, brought humanist ideas to North America.

The enduring legacy of humanism is that it transformed education and created a worldwide network of scholars with shared values and educational methods. Renaissance humanism eventually gave way to the era of increased specialization which emerged with the scientific and industrial revolutions of the sixteenth to nineteenth centuries. Yet even today, the study of the humanities retains its place in colleges and universities, since human beings will never lose interest in studying what it means to be human.

3

Roots of the Reformation

In the last chapter, I asserted that there are periods in history whose beginning and ending dates cannot be easily identified. In this chapter, I add a corollary notion that few, if any, historical events occur without some foundation or precedent in the past, even those eras whose beginning and ending dates can be clearly defined. I will also discuss in this chapter that, viewed in its historical context, Luther's posting of his *Ninety-five Theses* was pivotal but not unprecedented, and that the roots of the Reformation go back centuries before 1517.

There is a consensus among historians that the beginning of the Reformation period can be easily fixed to a particular day— October 31, 1517,[6] the eve of All Saints' Day, or Hallows' Eve— on which Martin Luther posted (or made public in some manner) his *Ninety-five Theses*. Yet the roots of the Reformation can be traced back centuries prior to this date. Likewise, historians have

---

[6] October 31 is celebrated annually by some Protestant churches as Reformation Day.

proposed suitable ending dates for the Reformation, such as the Peace of Augsburg (September 25, 1555); the beginning of the Thirty Years' War (May 23, 1618); and the signing of the Treaty of Westphalia (October 24, 1648), which ended the Thirty Years' War. Yet there is no consensus among historians on an ending date for the Reformation, and the consequences of this era are still with us today. This ambiguity demonstrates that while categories and divisions are necessary for understanding our world, assigning beginning and ending dates to historical periods is, to some extent, artificial. Further, the practice can be misleading if it is perceived to bracket or separate the events of those periods from what preceded and followed them. We must be ever mindful of the continuity of history and resist the urge to compartmentalize too much, since this will invariably mask the essential complexity of reality. Our aim should always be to contextualize.

With this in mind, Luther's posting of his *Ninety-five Theses* should be viewed as part of a progression of events and the continuation (and perhaps culmination) of the work of previous reform-minded thinkers rather than as an unprecedented break with the past. By underscoring the notion that nothing in history occurs without precedent and that everything has roots in the past, I do not mean to support a deterministic view of history or one that relies on fate. Free will and self-determination always play a role in human actions and history. Martin Luther did not assemble all of the kindling and firewood that became the great conflagration of the Reformation, but he did light the match.

~

To understand the roots of the Reformation, we must go back to Constantine the Great (r. 306–337) who became the sole emperor of the western half of the Roman Empire after marching his legions from Britain and Gaul to the outskirts of Rome and, on October 28, 312, defeated Maxentius at the Battle of the Milvian Bridge. A year later, he met with Licinius, the emperor of the eastern half of the Roman Empire, and they signed the Edict of Milan, or the Edict of Toleration (313), which granted religious freedom to everyone within the empire, including Christians. Although Constantine was not baptized until he was close to death, he began a policy during his long reign of favoring the Christian Church and fostering its growth.

Constantine followed up his victory in 312 by defeating Licinius at the Battle of Chrysopolis in 324. In the same year, he moved the capital of the unified Roman world from Rome to Byzantium, a town strategically located on the western side of the Bosporus, and named it (not surprisingly) Constantinople. This is the origin of the Byzantine Empire, or the Eastern Roman Empire, which outlived its western neighbor by a thousand years. Historians by convention often date the end of the western half of the Roman Empire to 476 when the last Roman Emperor, Romulus Augustulus (a boy at the time), was deposed by Odoacer, the first barbarian king of Italy. The demise of the Eastern Roman Empire can be easily dated to 1453 when the Ottoman Turks captured Constantinople.

After Constantine legalized Christianity in 313, he passed legislation that strengthened the Church and then initiated a policy that made it instrumental in his government—a policy of integration he expanded after defeating Licinius in 324. It was a monumental accomplishment to have won control of both halves of the empire, but an equally monumental task to govern it in peace. Christianity offered Constantine a means of promoting political stability and unifying the lands under his control, and the Church became akin to a "department" within his government. With this newfound prominence came wealth and "vocations." The number of Christians increased when it became safe to be Christian, and service in the Church became a desirable career, even for those who were less spiritually minded. Worldly souls with little interest in the mission of the Church inevitably attained positions of power, and with this came a measure of secularization. Constantine's use of Christianity as a means of unifying his vast empire was significant to the roots of the Reformation because it associated the Church in the affairs of state for the first time and set a precedent for the Church's involvement in temporal governance.

As the Church spread throughout Europe and barbarian tribes were brought into the Christian fold, the need for clergy as pastors and administrators increased. After the decline of the western provinces and the sack of Rome in 410, the remnants of the once-mighty Western Empire came under the control of barbarian kings. The feudal system developed in the absence of an official government, and along with the Church, the landed aristocracy became its central governing institution. Sons of wealthy landowners who were not destined to inherit their father's estates could pursue a career as a knight or opt for a career in the Church, which offered a viable career path not only to the aristocracy but to peasants as well. Employment in the Church could be prestigious and lucrative, and powerful lords often had their sons appointed to high ecclesiastical positions, even at a very young age. Churchmen who had offspring also engaged in this kind of nepotism, even with children who were born out of wedlock. Secularism and nepotism were widespread and perennial causes of scandal among the faithful during the Middle Ages, and these and other practices such as simony (the buying and selling of Church benefices) prompted calls for reform.

The Reformation of 1517 can be more directly traced to the beginning of the High Middle Ages (c. 1000–c. 1300), specifically to the papacy of the reforming pope, Gregory VII (r. 1073–1085). Gregory began his rule less than twenty years after the beginning of the Great Schism (1054) which split Christianity between the Eastern Church (Greek) and the Western Church (Latin). The rift was ostensibly over theological doctrine, particularly the longstanding dispute of whether the Holy Spirit descended "from the Father" (Greek Church) or "from the Father and the Son" (Latin Church)—a dispute summed up in the Latin term *Filioque* ("and the Son"). The real cause of the schism, however, was more about authority than doctrine, and whether the pope had primacy over the patriarch of Constantinople. Today we know these churches as the Eastern Orthodox Church and the Roman Catholic Church.

Gregory (b. 1025) had been active in Church administration from the beginning of his ecclesiastical career and was heavily influenced if not scarred by this unfortunate event. As a result, a key element of his reforms was his insistence on papal primacy, not only over other bishops and patriarchs but also over kings and nobles. Royalty and nobility had acquired over the centuries the prerogative of appointing Church officials, including bishops and abbots who governed territories—a practice known as "lay investiture." Gregory, however, banned this practice, which significantly increased the power of the pope and brought unprecedented unity and centralization to the medieval Latin Church, even if it initiated a long and arduous struggle that would extend far beyond his reign. He also insisted on the enforcement of canon law, which eventually became an international law, and issued decrees against simony and clerical marriage. As expected, his reforms were met with widespread resistance.

Gregory VII's successors continued his policy of centralizing Church authority and increasing papal power by assuming the mantle of monarchy. By attempting to establish their vision of a Christian empire (Christendom) modeled on ancient Rome with the pope as its supreme head, they put themselves in direct competition for worldly power with kings and feudal lords. This was not entirely unreasonable or unwarranted, however, since the Church was a civilizing force during the Middle Ages and served as a check and balance on the power of kings and nobles who routinely warred against each other, used the Church for their own aggrandizement, and often mistreated peasants. Additionally, in the absence of a system of state-run education, the Church founded schools and the first universities, and monasteries produced and preserved books, housed libraries, and were centers of learning. Educated churchmen often served as tutors to the youth of royalty and nobility, and the Church was counted on to supply a cadre of capable leaders and administrators who governed in coordination with secular rulers.

Pope Innocent III (r. 1198–1216), the next reforming pope after Gregory and perhaps the most powerful leader of his day, expanded the idea of papal monarchy and the doctrine that the pope's power comes directly from God, reformed the Roman Curia, refined canon law, and vigorously attempted to stamp out heresy. Regrettably, he called the Fourth Crusade that ended with the infamous sack of Constantinople (which he strongly opposed, writing explicit instructions to the Crusaders beforehand ordering them not to do it and then excommunicating them afterward). To his credit, however, he permitted Saint Dominic (1170–1221) and Saint Francis of Assisi (1181–1226)—also important reform-minded thinkers—to found new mendicant religious orders. He also convened the Fourth Lateran Council in 1215, confirmed the fundamental doctrine on the Eucharist, issued important reformatory decrees, and ordered that all Christians confess their sins once a year to a priest.

The reforms of Gregory VII and Innocent III and their example of strong papal leadership brought mixed blessings and unintended consequences. As the Church progressively became more centralized, organized, and bureaucratically efficient, it also became wealthier and more powerful, which led to greater materialism and worldliness. Popes began to model their courts on those of secular kings and eventually tried to eclipse them in splendor, which caused widespread scandal among the faithful. Yet as the Church's coffers filled with gold and its leaders indulged in sumptuous lifestyles, many wealthy landowners concerned about their eternal salvation bequeathed land and other property to the Church before their death in exchange for Requiem Masses, prayers, and benefits they hoped to receive in eternity. Since the Church was able to possess these lands in perpetuity, it eventually became one of the wealthiest landholders in Europe—a status which caused anxiety to kings and other secular rulers.

Anticlerical sentiments and discontent were amplified during the mid-fourteenth century when the spiritual power of the Church proved ineffective in alleviating the catastrophe of the Black Death (1347–1351). The reputation of the Church suffered further damage during the prolonged residence of the pope at Avignon, whose lavish papal palace, constructed at great expense, caused further scandal among the faithful. Papal residence in a city other than Rome would always be controversial, but Italian political factions and the unruly and sometimes violent Roman mob made papal elections in Rome difficult and often unfair. If the pope were to reside in Avignon, he needed a castle that provided safety from his political enemies and protected the treasure that was kept there, since the papal palace served not only as the pope's residence and official headquarters, but also as the international administrative center of the Church and its central banking office. The Avignon Papacy finally ended in 1377 when Pope Gregory XI returned the papal residence to Rome.

The Church's growth in power and wealth during the High and Late Middle Ages was facilitated by several important factors that tended to unify it across international boundaries and give it an advantage over secular rulers with whom it competed for power. These factors included:

1. Christianity had a thousand-year tradition upon which it could rely, a well-developed theology, and official sacraments, all of which provided religious unity and cohesion to the medieval world.

2. The Church in Europe was unified under a common tongue, as Latin served as an international language in matters both secular and sacred.[7]

3. Canon law became an international law recognized throughout Europe (we will examine this in a later chapter).

4. The Church advanced civilization and promoted education, and its hierarchy consisted of a professional class of priests, many of whom could read and write, and some were highly educated.

---

[7] Thomas More and Desiderius Erasmus, for example, were good friends but could only communicate with each other in Latin.

5. Territories governed by secular rulers (such as kingdoms, duchies, and principalities) were restricted by geographical boundaries, and the reigns of kings and nobles were limited by their lifespans and the duration of their dynasties. Conversely, the Church under an elected pope was an international and perpetual institution endowed with a unique continuity that enabled it to own property and govern lands from century to century.

Advantages not properly utilized can become weaknesses, however, and the wealth and power of the Church tended to insulate it from the need to amend its moral and financial abuses. Despite enduring calls for reform, the Church continued to generate a substantial income through donations and the collection of tithes, taxes, and fees for an assortment of rights and privileges, including the granting of benefices (simony). And while it must be conceded that an ample income is necessary to operate a multinational organization as large as the Church, the opulent lifestyles of some in its hierarchy caused public scandal. In addition, the Church's steadfast resistance to secular taxation was resented by kings, lords, and peasants alike, some of whom regretted the drain of wealth to a foreign pope whose interests were not always their own. This resentment only deepened because of the special privileges granted to clerics, monks, nuns, and friars—such as exemptions from military service and other civic duties required of ordinary citizens. Worse still, popes and bishops frequently intervened in secular matters (not always unjustly), and there was no shortage of clerics and professed religious who caused public scandal by their sexual immorality and worldliness.

Another problem that harmed the reputation of the Church was the unfit and uneducated men who were sometimes ordained to the priesthood, some of whom were barely literate and knew only enough Latin to stumble through the Mass. Many of these were poorly paid and served as cheap labor for bishops and archbishops (often from aristocratic families) who received income from these benefices but lived elsewhere (absenteeism). According to canon law, a clergyman was permitted one benefice where he was required to reside, but dispensations for plurality (multiple benefices) and nonresidence[8] were frequently granted for a fee. Some prelates amassed great fortunes from multiple benefices and lived in magnificent palaces and estates. In brief, pluralism, absenteeism, simony, secularism, worldliness, greed, venality, materialism, nepotism, hypocrisy, and the casual disregard for celibacy were the principal moral and financial abuses of the Church during the pre-Reformation era and were not adequately addressed until the Counter-Reformation that began with the first session of the Council of Trent in 1545.

The popes of the fifteenth and sixteenth centuries were presented with yet another difficult problem, the solution of which caused much indignation and contributed greatly to the Reformation of 1517. The original Saint Peter's Basilica built by

---

[8] Some clerics never even visited their benefices but collected the income anyway.

Emperor Constantine in the fourth century had begun to fall into ruin, and the only viable option available to architects at that time was to demolish it before it collapsed. The pope certainly needed a safe home and a secure administrative headquarters, but it was also deemed fitting that the center of the Latin Church be adorned with attractive art and elegant architecture and display some sense of grandeur. The resources needed to rebuild Saint Peter's Basilica and the funds desired by the Renaissance popes to support the arts were acquired in part through the collection of money from the granting of indulgences. The first indulgence (known as the "Crusader indulgence") was offered by Pope Urban II in 1095 as an incentive for nobles and knights to travel to the Holy Land and do battle to regain Christian holy sites from the Muslims. The practice was later extended to those who would support a Crusader, and eventually indulgences were offered to those who could only pray, do good works, and tithe. During the early sixteenth century, papal preachers were collecting alms for the reconstruction of Saint Peter's Basilica and offering indulgences in return. Yet there is an important distinction between: (a) "granting" indulgences to those who pray, fast, give alms, and do good works, and (b) "selling" indulgences as a way of making money—and it was this issue that finally prompted Martin Luther to take that fateful step on October 31, 1517 that forever changed the world.

~

I wrote above that Luther's posting of his *Ninety-five Theses* should be viewed as part of a progression of historical events and the continuation of the work of previous reform-minded thinkers rather than as an unprecedented break with the past. If the roots of the Reformation can be loosely traced to Constantine in the fourth century, and more directly to the reform-minded popes and founders of new religious orders of the High Middle Ages, then these roots can most directly be traced to the important early reformers who preceded and tangibly contributed to the Reformation of 1517. These include:

- Peter Waldo (1140–1218), a merchant from Lyon and a contemporary of Innocent III, Dominic, and Francis. Waldo is credited with having founded a lay religious institute originally known as the Poor of Lyon and later as the Waldensians. Not much is known about him except that he is said to have been attracted to holy poverty as was Francis, but he preached heretical doctrine and he and his followers were excommunicated. The Waldensians aligned themselves with Protestantism during the sixteenth century and they can still be found today in parts of Europe and the Americas.

- Marsilius of Padua (1275–1342), who wrote *Defensor Pacis* (1324), an influential treatise on theology and political philosophy which challenged papal authority. He was declared a heretic in 1327.

- The English Franciscan, William of Ockham (1287–1347), who endorsed the philosophy of nominalism, which denies the existence of forms and essences—key concepts on which the theology of the Church is based. Ockham and the nominalists taught that reality consists of individual beings, and that universal concepts such as forms and essences are merely ideas in the human mind. He also proposed a political philosophy that included the separation between Church and state, each with its own sphere—the Church as ruler in the spiritual realm and the state in the secular realm. Further, he argued that Church officials should pay taxes and be subject to secular courts, which King Henry VIII of England would insist upon two hundred years later. William was in Avignon in 1328 meeting with the pope and his representatives, but he fled the city when he realized his life was in danger and was excommunicated.

- John Wycliffe (1330–1384), a notable precursor to the English Reformation that began under Henry VIII, was an English priest and professor at the university in Oxford. Trained as a scholastic, he deplored along with many of his countrymen the rule of a foreign papacy and the worldliness and materialism of the Church. To remedy its financial abuses, Wycliffe proposed that clerics and religious orders adopt voluntary poverty or be disendowed by the king and nobles. In the political sphere, Wycliffe championed the king's rights over the pope's and declared that clerics should not hold high offices in secular governments. These ideas would later influence Henry VIII and provide him with moral and legal justification for asserting the king's authority in England over the pope's and the superiority of common law over canon law. Wycliffe was also the first to translate the Bible from the Latin Vulgate into English, and he criticized the Church's theology, most notably the authenticity of the papacy, the necessity of the priesthood, and the doctrine of transubstantiation. Wycliffe was declared a heretic in 1415.

- John Hus (1369–1415), a priest and theologian, was a reformer in the mold of William of Ockham. Like many of his predecessors, he denounced the immorality of the clergy, and in anticipation of Martin Luther, he preached against indulgences. Hus' ideas gained widespread popularity in Bohemia, and he was invited to the Council of Constance (1414–1418) to explain his positions. Guaranteed safe conduct by King Sigismund, he was betrayed, tried, convicted of heresy, and burned at the stake. This caused a revolt in Bohemia that led to the Hussite Wars (1419–1434). Jerome of Prague, also of Bohemia, was executed a year after Hus's death.

- Desiderius Erasmus (1466–1536) of Rotterdam and William Tyndale (1494–1536) of England were influential reform-minded thinkers who lived during the Reformation period beginning in 1517. Tyndale translated the New Testament and parts of the Old Testament from the original Hebrew and Greek into English; he was condemned as a heretic and executed in 1536. Erasmus, on the other hand, was a good friend of More's and a fellow humanist and was never tainted by a charge of heresy or excommunicated.

4

The Wars of the Roses

The length of the Hundred Years' War and any hope the kings of England had of obtaining the throne of France were made possible only by the persistent disunity that plagued France's nobility during the fourteenth and fifteenth centuries. This discord reached a low point during the reign of King Charles VI of France (r. 1380–1422) and the civil war that erupted between the houses of Burgundy and Orléans. Had France been united under a French king and had it been able to concentrate a portion of its military and economic resources on the war effort, it would have easily fended off English encroachments and perhaps invaded England itself. But once King Charles VII and the Duke of Burgundy resolved their differences after the death of the Duke of Bedford's wife (the sister of the Duke of Burgundy) in 1432 and Bedford's death in 1435, Philip of Burgundy abandoned his alliance with the English. The path was now open to a unified France under a French king, and victory over the English was possible.

Perhaps it was divine irony or an improbable twist of fate that at Bedford's passing and the reconciliation between Charles VII and Burgundy, some of the most powerful nobles in England became entangled in a dispute of their own over whether to continue the war in France. Had Henry V lived a full life, this dynastic struggle between two branches of the royal Plantagenet family which had ruled England for the past three hundred years would not have occurred. There would have been no peace party and Henry V might have fulfilled his quest to unite all of England and France under one kingship. But Henry died in 1422 at age thirty-five from dysentery, and his heir was a mere infant without the gifts of character and constitution nature had bestowed on his father in abundance. Henry VI (r. 1422–1461; 1470–1471) was destined for the throne of England but could never fill it in the manner his father had, and the power vacuum that ensued—initially from his youth and later his absence of leadership—resulted in a competition for power among England's leading nobles.

The origin of this feud between the houses of Lancaster and York can be traced to the death of Bedford in 1435. Henry VI was only fourteen years old when his capable uncle passed away, and the peace party was able to convince Parliament to reduce war expenditures. In doing so, they made an enemy of Richard, Duke of York, who was commanding the English army in France. In 1445, the Duke of Suffolk, a member of the peace party, arranged a marriage between the twenty-three-year-old Henry VI and the fourteen-year-old daughter of the Duke of Anjou. What he could not have foreseen, however, was Margaret's headstrong and domineering personality and the effect this would have on the political situation in England. Margaret's ambition and jealousy of her rights as queen thoroughly prevailed over her gentle and over-matched royal husband. She desired to end the war in France—which was one reason she was selected to be the king's bride by Suffolk and the peace party—but her determination to destroy her Yorkist enemies eventually resulted in armed conflict between the houses of Lancaster and York and the nobles who were allied with them. The Wars of the Roses is traditionally dated from 1455 to 1485, but its roots can be traced to the death of Bedford in 1435 and the marriage of Henry and Margaret in 1445.

In order to obtain the consent of King Charles VII of France to the marriage of Henry and Margaret, the Duke of Suffolk agreed to withdraw English troops from Le Maine. In 1447, the Duke of Gloucester—uncle of Henry VI and one of the leaders of the war party—learned of the plan to give Le Maine to the French and bitterly repudiated it as a betrayal of England's national interests. In a fit of anger, he spoke rashly and was arrested and murdered a few days later. Suspicion fell on Queen Margaret. That same year, Henry Beaufort, Bishop of Winchester, died, and leadership of the peace party (which had become the queen's party) passed to Edmund Beaufort, Duke of Somerset, and William de la Pole, Duke of Suffolk. Since Henry VI was from the Lancastrian branch of the Plantagenet family, the peace party (or queen's party) became known as the Lancastrians. The war party was led by the Duke of York, but the queen's party had him removed from his command in France and sent to Ireland for a ten-year appointment as its lieutenant.

The return of Le Maine to the French in 1448 was viewed in England as a national disgrace and Queen Margaret became very unpopular among her subjects. King Charles VII renewed the war in France, and by 1450, England had lost all of its continental possessions except for Calais, Guyenne, and Gascony, causing public opinion to be heavily against the queen and her advisors. The Duke of Suffolk, matchmaker of Henry VI and Margaret, was intercepted at sea and executed. Jack Cade led a rebellion and marched on London, capturing it in July 1450. Cade was later executed, but dissatisfaction and uprisings spread throughout England. The Duke of York sailed home amid the calamity and Margaret, fearing the worst at the return of her enemy, sent agents to assassinate him; she also recalled Somerset from France. York landed safely, evaded Margaret's troops, and returned to his castle in Ludlow. No combat ensued, but the two rival factions stiffened, and like the sword of Damocles, the shadow of war loomed over England.

The deficiencies of a weak king and the vehemence of his passionate and improvident queen were on full display during the next five years. War had not yet broken out on English soil, but it was not long in the offing. The party that wanted peace in France and imported a strong-willed French noblewoman to assist their cause had gotten their wish, but the cost was steep. In 1453, the English were soundly defeated at the Battle of Castillon, which put an end to the Hundred Years' War. The public outrage caused Henry, who was unable to cope with the stress, to have a mental breakdown, and he was reduced to silence and incomprehension. Margaret gave birth to a son that same year, who may have been Henry's, but since the king was in poor mental health, it was presumed that Somerset fathered the child so that the queen's party might have an heir to Henry. The new prince, Edward, became the most valuable pawn in the Lancastrian game of thrones (aside from the king) and protected Margaret and Somerset's power, but they could not avert the ruling of Parliament, which appointed the Duke of York as Protector of England in 1454. Somerset was imprisoned in the Tower of London, but the king regained his senses and fell again under the power of his domineering spouse. York was forced to resign and Somerset was freed. Both sides marshaled their allies, and war had come to England.

The first battle of the Wars of the Roses occurred in May 1455 in the town of Saint Albans near London. It was the Duke of Somerset's last day on earth (and not among his happiest), and Henry VI was captured and led back to London by the victorious Duke of York. Margaret, fearing retribution or humiliation, fled with her son to the royal palace at Greenwich. Had she been a less determined, resourceful, and talented queen, or had she been willing to accept the lawful rulings of Parliament, hostilities might have ended then, a peace parley arranged, and the nobility of England reconciled. But Margaret, whose natural virtues of courage and fortitude were matched with a no less abundant self-will and vindictiveness, sought to regain control of the puppet-king Henry and the eventual destruction of her political enemies.

In 1459, the queen managed the remarkable feat of assembling an army and driving the Duke of York out of England along with his two oldest sons, Edward, Earl of March (1442–1483)[9] and Edmund, Earl of Rutland (1443–1460).[10] They were accompanied by their main allies, Richard Neville, Earl of Salisbury, and his son, Richard, Earl of Warwick. But the Yorkists were not away long enough for Margaret to consolidate her power, and in 1460, Warwick, Salisbury, and March returned from Calais and assembled an army of their own. On July 10, they met and defeated a Lancastrian force at the Battle of Northampton and once again captured the king. Margaret fled with Prince Edward from London and took refuge in the Welsh castle of Jasper Tudor, Earl of Pembroke and the half-brother of King Henry VI.[11]

York sailed from Ireland in October and returned to London while Parliament was in session, but his claim to the throne of England before its members in Westminster Hall (he was a descendant of Edward III) was not warmly received. Margaret was

---

[9] The future King Edward IV.

[10] Edmund was killed at the Battle of Wakefield in 1460. This Edmund should not be confused with Edmund Tudor, who was the father of the future King Henry VII.

[11] The Tudors were loyal to the Lancastrian cause. Henry Tudor (1457-1509), the future King Henry VII (r. 1485-1509), became the last surviving male in the Lancastrian line and the first Tudor king after his victory at the Battle of Bosworth Field in 1485.

highly unpopular, but not even York's allies desired to overthrow King Henry. A compromise was reached where Henry would remain king and York was named his successor, thus removing Prince Edward from the line of succession. Margaret would not relent, however. She assembled another army from the noble families in the north of England still loyal to the Lancastrian cause and took personal command of it. Among her other talents, she proved to be a capable military strategist and crushed a force led by York at the Battle of Wakefield on December 30, 1460. York and Rutland were killed in battle and Salisbury was later beheaded. Margaret, at least for the moment, had defied the odds and won, but the Wars of the Roses would last for another twenty-five years and it was marked by sudden and stunning reversals of fortune.

Richard of York's nineteen-year-old son, Edward, Earl of March, succeeded his father as the Duke of York, and he would prove to be the most competent commander on either side in the Wars of the Roses. He won his first victory in 1461 at the Battle of Mortimer's Cross in Wales against a Lancastrian army led by Jasper Tudor,[12] but Margaret crushed an army led by Warwick at the Second Battle of Saint Albans. Warwick had brought the king with him as he marched north from London, and his defeat caused Henry to fall again into the queen's hands. Margaret

---

[12] Jasper's father, Owen Tudor, fought on the Lancastrian side and was beheaded after the battle. Owen Tudor was also the father of Edmund Tudor, who was the father of Henry Tudor, the future King Henry VII. Edmund Tudor died in 1456 from the bubonic plague, which is why Henry Tudor was raised by his uncle, Jasper.

marched her army south to London in triumph, but the city would not open its gates to her because she was so unpopular and for fear of her unruly northern soldiers. She had little choice but to return to northern England.

In February 1461, Edward, Earl of March, arrived at London with his army and was greeted with cheers. Henry was declared unfit for the crown on March 1 and Edward proclaimed himself king three days later. The mood had shifted in London and Edward's bid for the crown, unlike his father's, was well received. Edward wasted no time pursuing Margaret and marched an army north to prevent her from reaching Scotland. Warwick traveled with him, along with Lord Fauconberg and many others loyal to the Yorkist cause. Fighting on the Lancastrian side were Henry Percy, Earl of Northumberland, Henry Beaufort, Duke of Somerset, and nobles from the Tudor and Clifford families. The Battle of Towton was fought in a snowstorm on March 29, 1461, and was decided by the Duke of Norfolk who arrived late in the day with an army from Kent to tilt the battle in the Yorkists' favor.

It was the bloodiest battle ever fought on English soil. The king, queen, and prince were not present on the battlefield, but waited instead in York for the outcome. When they heard of the defeat, they fled to Scotland with the Duke of Somerset. Edward of March spent the next few months subduing the north of England and then returned to London in June to be crowned King

Edward IV (r. 1461–1483).[13] His right to rule was confirmed by Parliament, but the indomitable Margaret was busy collecting allies in Scotland and France. Her efforts to invade England in 1462 with a Scottish and French army and reinvigorate her support among the northern nobles were severely hampered by bad luck and poor weather. Margaret was forced to flee to France in 1462 and her ally, the Duke of Somerset, was captured near Hexham in 1464 and beheaded. Henry VI was captured by Edward's forces near Clitheroe in Lancashire in 1465 and carted off to be imprisoned in the Tower of London. Edward IV made peace with France and Burgundy, but Margaret had not yet played her last card.

The war should have ended with the defeat of the Lancastrian forces and the death of many of their nobles, but it instead entered a new phase as Edward began to rule as king alongside his wealthy, powerful, and self-interested ally, the Earl of Warwick. Edward was still a young man in his early twenties, and Warwick was fourteen years his senior. Despite Warwick's efforts to find him a bride within France's royal family, Edward, to everyone's great surprise, secretly married Elizabeth Woodville in May 1464. This humiliated and infuriated Warwick. To make matters worse, Edward granted land and titles to members of the Woodville family, causing indignation among England's nobility.

---

[13] Edward IV's rule was interrupted in 1470-1471 when Henry VI was briefly restored to the throne.

By 1469, Warwick could suffer the outrage no longer. Contrary to Edward's wishes, he conspired with Edward's brother, Clarence, to have him marry Warwick's daughter, Isobel, in Calais. He further planned to discredit Edward as an illegitimate son and put Clarence on the throne in his place. Many nobles who resented Edward's presumptuous generosity towards the Woodvilles joined Warwick and Clarence to defeat and execute a few of Edward's important allies. The king himself was captured and Warwick began to rule in Edward's name, but many of the nobles distrusted him and refused to send troops to put down another Lancastrian revolt in the north. Warwick had no better option than to set Edward free.

The betrayal would not be forgotten. In 1470, Edward gathered an army and marched against Warwick and Clarence, forcing them to flee to France. There they devised a plan with King Louis XI to put Henry VI back on the throne, but this would require an improbable alliance between Warwick and Margaret. When first presented with the idea, Margaret refused, but she was nevertheless persuaded to at least meet with Warwick. On July 22, the once mortal enemies met, and the seething Margaret, with Prince Edward present, agreed to the plan.

Warwick and Clarence returned to England while Margaret waited in France. The earl commanded an army composed of disaffected Lancastrians, forces loyal to him, and French soldiers on loan from Louis XI. He landed in England in 1470, and in the ever-shifting alliances among the English nobility during the Wars of the Roses, Edward was compelled to flee to Flanders and then Burgundy. In another remarkable reversal of fortune, Henry VI was restored to the throne and the Lancastrians regained power. Their victory would be short-lived, however.

In November, England and France declared war on Burgundy, which Warwick and Clarence had previously agreed to in exchange for Louis XI's assistance in restoring Henry VI to the throne. This forced Charles, Duke of Burgundy, into an alliance with Edward IV. Edward was given Burgundian soldiers and sailed for England in March 1471, and received an additional boost when Clarence changed sides and returned to his brother. Edward immediately marched to London and was again warmly received by its citizenry, but he wasted no time and marched his army north the next day to settle the matter with Warwick and his allies. Accompanying Edward into battle were Clarence, Richard Plantagenet, Duke of Gloucester,[14] and William, Lord Hastings. On April 14, Easter Sunday, Edward defeated Warwick at the Battle of Barnet, and the earl was rewarded for his treachery by being slain as he fled the battlefield.

Margaret and the seventeen-year-old Prince Edward landed in England before they heard of the defeat. Margaret could have returned to France but chose instead to travel north with Somerset to recruit another army and confront Edward IV's battered troops. Edward learned of her arrival and intercepted her before she and her forces could get to safety and defeated her at

---

[14] The future King Richard III.

the Battle of Tewkesbury on May 4, 1471. Prince Edward was killed, and Henry VI's heir was no longer a factor. Margaret hid but was captured and brought to London, her liberty later purchased by the King of France for a large ransom. Somerset was beheaded after the battle by Richard, Duke of Gloucester, and Henry VI was again imprisoned in the Tower. The pendulum of dynastic struggle had swung again, this time toward the Yorkists.

Henry VI conveniently passed away on May 21, 1471. It was said that he died of sadness, although the cause of his death is still not known. It is certain, however, that his death and the demise of his princely son sealed Edward's victory and his claim to the throne, and it is possible that his "passing" may have been prematurely hastened to ensure no further rebellion. In any event, England spent the remaining years of Edward's reign in peace. Margaret of Anjou died in 1482, alone and in virtual poverty. Edward died a successful king in 1483. But the Wars of the Roses was not over, and the pendulum would swing again, this time away from the House of York and toward the House of Lancaster— to a sole survivor who would become king and unite both houses in marriage.

And another dynasty of illustrious fame would be born.

5

The House of Tudor

Henry V of England married Catherine of Valois (1401–1437) in 1420, and the only child she bore him before he died of dysentery in 1422 was Henry VI. Seven years after Henry V's death, Queen Catherine married a Welsh squire named Sir Owen Tudor (1400–1461), which meant that any offspring she bore him would be maternal half-siblings of Henry VI. Owen Tudor became the grandfather of Henry VII (Henry Tudor) through Catherine, which meant that Catherine was the mother of Henry VI by Henry V, and the grandmother of Henry VII by Owen Tudor. The Tudor dynasty, which began in 1485 with Henry VII, lasted until the death of Queen Elizabeth I in 1603.

Owen Tudor and Queen Catherine had at least two sons, Edmund (1430–1456) and Jasper (1431–1495). In 1442, Henry VI invited his half-brothers to live at his royal court where they were educated and received military training. The king later ennobled them, and in 1455, Edmund, now Earl of Richmond, married Margaret Beaufort, who bore him Henry Tudor (1457–1509), the future King Henry VII. Edmund was captured by Yorkist forces in 1456 and imprisoned at Carmarthen Castle where he died from the bubonic plague three months before Henry was born. Since Margaret was only thirteen years old, Henry Tudor was brought into the household of his uncle Jasper, Earl of Pembroke, and raised there.

Jasper commanded the Lancastrian army at the Battle of Mortimer's Cross in 1461 and was defeated by Edward, Duke of York (the future King Edward IV). Owen Tudor also fought on the Lancastrian side, survived the battle, but was subsequently captured and beheaded. When Edward IV became king in 1461, Jasper fled to France and remained there for six years under the protection of King Louis XI. His nephew, Henry Tudor, remained at Pembroke Castle with his mother, Margaret, under the guardianship of the Yorkist, William Herbert, the new Earl of Pembroke.

In 1469, Richard Neville, Earl of Warwick, switched sides, betrayed Edward IV, and began fighting for the Lancastrians and the restoration of Henry VI (who became king again in 1470). Jasper Tudor returned briefly to England but fled again to Brittany with his nephew Henry and other Lancastrians in 1471 when Edward IV regained the throne. Jasper remained in France for the remainder of Edward's reign working on behalf of the Lancastrian cause and its sole remaining male heir, Henry Tudor, Earl of Richmond. Edward, for his part, sought to have Jasper and Henry repatriated to England, but they were protected by Francis II, Duke of Brittany.

Edward IV died in 1483, and on his deathbed, he named his brother, Richard, Duke of Gloucester (1452–1485), as Lord Protector of Edward's son and heir, Edward V (1470–1483). This disrupted the Woodville's plans of controlling the young king, and when Richard gained custody of Edward and his brother, Richard, Duke of York (1473–1483), he placed them in the Tower of London. Richard then worked to discredit Edward's marriage to Elizabeth Woodville by claiming that Edward had been previously married to another woman, and that his marriage to Elizabeth was therefore invalid and their sons illegitimate. This would prevent them from inheriting the throne and create an avenue for Richard, as the dead king's brother, to claim it for himself. Richard III (r. 1483–1485) was crowned in Westminster Abbey on July 6, 1483, but his position was not entirely secure since Edward's sons were still alive and, with the help of the Woodvilles and their allies, they might someday contest his kingship.

In Sir Thomas More's *The History of King Richard III*, which he wrote in the early 1500s and not long after the events that concluded the Wars of the Roses, More states that Richard III sent Sir James Tyrell to London to murder the two boys while they were still lodged in the Tower, and that Tyrell recruited two other men, John Dighton and Miles Forest, to enter their room at night and smother them with their pillows while Tyrell stood guard at the door. According to More, they buried the bodies at the foot of a staircase—an account that is corroborated by the discovery of a wooden chest in 1674 containing the bones of two children found at the foot of a staircase by workmen who were remodeling the Tower of London. Those bones have resided in a monument in Westminster Abbey since 1678.

There is no definitive proof that Richard III had the princes murdered and the matter is still disputed today, but rumors circulated at that time that he was responsible for their deaths. The scandal created division even within the Yorkist party and Richard became unpopular among the nobility and commoners alike, even in an age when the execution of one's enemies was routine. The murder of the princes is considered one of the most infamous acts in English royal history and notoriety has surrounded Richard's name since.

Richard III would rule for two anxious years. Like Edward IV before him, Richard wanted Jasper and Henry Tudor returned to England from Brittany so he could eliminate them as the only remaining Lancastrian threats. Duke Francis, however, would not hand them over. In 1483, the Duke of Buckingham attempted a rebellion that was supposed to be coordinated with a Lancastrian invasion from Brittany, but the plan failed and Buckingham was executed. Richard moved to have Jasper and Henry Tudor extradited from Brittany in 1484, but a plot he devised with Pierre Landais, Francis's chief administrator, was foiled and Jasper and Henry fled to the protection of the fourteen-year-old French king, Charles VIII. They remained there until 1485 when, aided by the French, they landed a small army in Wales on August 7 and marched into England. Henry's French and Scottish soldiers were joined by Welshmen eager to fight, and Henry moved quickly to engage Richard. Their armies met on August 22, and Henry defeated Richard at the Battle of Bosworth Field. Richard was killed while fighting bravely in battle, and according to legend, Henry VII (r. 1485–1509) was crowned at the place where Richard fell with the crown the dead king wore into battle.

The Wars of the Roses ended with the Battle of Bosworth Field and with it the Plantagenet dynasty. On January 18, 1486, Henry VII married Elizabeth of York, the daughter of Edward IV and Elizabeth Woodville, thus uniting the houses of Lancaster and York and inaugurating the Tudor dynasty that lasted until 1603.

~

Henry VIII's desire for a male heir must be understood in the context of the Wars of the Roses and its aftermath. It was surely a matter of anxiety for Henry VIII that in the absence of a clear, undisputed heir to the throne, multiple claimants might step forth and trigger another protracted power struggle that could result in war. Understanding motivations does not always allow us to justify actions, but it does give us perspective and greater insight into the historical situation.

Part Two

God's Good Servant
and the King's

Oh, how I love your law!
    It is my meditation all day long.
Your command makes me wiser than my enemies;
    for it is always with me.
I have more understanding than all my teachers,
    for your decrees are my meditation.
I understand more than the aged,
    for I keep your precepts.

Psalm 119:97–100

6

A Hero is Chosen
Son of a Barrister (1478 to 1484)

John More and Agnes Graunger were married on April 24, 1474, in Saint Giles Church in Cripplegate. They welcomed their first child, Joan, into the world on March 11, 1475, and their first son on February 7, 1478. He was baptized and given the name "Thomas" as had many other English sons since Thomas Becket's martyrdom in 1170,[15] but Thomas More would share more than a first name with one of England's most venerated and beloved saints. Becket was born on the corner of Ironmonger Lane and Cheapside, a mere twenty yards from the More family home on Milk Street in the prosperous ward of Cripplegate. Becket's original home had been replaced by a church named in his honor which More passed every day on his way to and from elementary school. There were probably other boys in the Cripplegate

---

[15] The popularity of the name "Thomas" in More's day is evidenced by the fact that at least six of Henry VIII's ministers shared it: (1) Thomas Wolsey, (2) Thomas Cromwell, (3) Thomas Howard, (4) Thomas Wriothesley, (5) Thomas Cranmer, and (6) Thomas More.

neighborhood named "Thomas" and certainly others in London, but unlike these, Becket and More would share the two finer distinctions of martyrdom and sainthood: Both were martyred under an English king named "Henry"—Becket by Henry II (r. 1154–1189) and More by Henry VIII (r. 1509–1547); and both were canonized—Becket in 1173 and More in 1935.[16]

John More was twenty-seven years old when Thomas was born and had for some years been climbing in rank at Lincoln's Inn and advancing his career as a lawyer. Agnes would bear John four more children before dying in 1499. Thomas More did not speak much about his siblings later in life, and records from this era are incomplete, but we know that Thomas's older sister, Joan (1475–1542), married a lawyer, Richard Staverton, as did his younger sister, Elizabeth (1482–1538), who married John Rastell.[17] Thomas' younger brother, John (1479–1512), also lived into adulthood and was periodically employed by Thomas as a secretary, but he never married and died in his early thirties. There is no record of the lives or deaths of their other two siblings— Agatha (b. 1479) and Edward (b. 1480)—except that they died young, but we know that Agnes gave birth to her last child in 1482 (Elizabeth), and in 1479 and 1485, London experienced outbreaks of contagion known as the "English sweat" or "sweating

---

[16] More was canonized exactly four hundred years after his martyrdom (1535–1935), and Becket only three (1170–1173).

[17] John and Elizabeth had a son, William Rastell, who edited and printed the English works of Thomas More in 1557 and wrote a biography of his famous uncle, most of which has not survived.

sickness." This illness (one of the few things Henry VIII feared) may have claimed their lives, or they may have perished in the plague that visited London in 1487. In any case, John More remarried three times after Agnes' death, but it is not likely that his other wives bore him any children.

Before his marriage to Agnes in 1474, More was employed at Lincoln's Inn, and by 1478, he had ascended from Master of the Revels to Butler to Marshal, all of which were important administrative posts that were essential for the proper functioning of the Inn. The duties of the Master of the Revels, for example, far from being trifling or servile, were so important that Thomas More accepted the position when he was Lord Chancellor of England and at the height of his power.

John More was also a landowner by inheritance, which enhanced his status in English society as a landed gentleman. He and Agnes owned a house in Cripplegate and property in Hertfordshire. More was eventually admitted to the Bar and performed his duties as a barrister so well that in 1503, he was promoted to the rank of serjeant-at-law (approximately equivalent to the status of a knight and, along with judges, the most senior level of barristers in England at this time). From this position at Serjeants' Inn, he ascended to sit as a judge in the Court of Common Pleas before reaching the summit of his career as a judge in the Court of the King's Bench. When Sir Thomas More was Lord Chancellor of England, it was his duty to preside over the Court of Chancery at Westminster Hall, which also housed the

Court of the King's Bench, and when "Young More" encountered his father in the public halls, amidst all of the bustle and busyness of the workday, he would fall to his knees before him as a sign of respect and ask for his blessing.

7

Early Years and Education (1484 to 1502)

It cannot be said that Thomas More's path to royal service began from the humblest of origins. John More enrolled his son at Saint Anthony's School on Threadneedle Street, the finest of London's four or five elementary schools, and even though it was the only one that offered free admission, it provided Thomas with a primary education second to none. The chief benefit of a "grammar school" of this kind was that students learned to read, write, and speak in Latin—the lingua franca of Europe. Proficiency in Latin was necessary not only for a career in the Church but for one in the common law courts and government as well, and the boys were expected to converse in Latin as fluently as in English.

More attended Saint Anthony's School for five years. At age twelve, his father arranged for him to become a page in the household of John Morton, Archbishop of Canterbury and Lord Chancellor of England under King Henry VII. Morton had been faithful to the Lancastrian cause during the Wars of the Roses and went into exile in France when Edward IV became king. He reconciled with the Yorkists only after Henry VI and his heir were dead, but he served Edward as faithfully as he did the Lancastrians—first as Bishop of Ely and later as a member of Edward's Privy Council. When Edward died and Richard III usurped the throne, Richard had Morton imprisoned in the castle of the Duke of Buckingham, who later began a revolt against Richard but was captured and executed. Morton survived the ordeal and was rewarded for his faithfulness to the Lancastrian cause after Henry Tudor defeated Richard at the Battle of Bosworth Field. Henry VII installed Morton as the Archbishop of Canterbury and later as Lord Chancellor of England. It was a testament to Morton's competence and skill as an administrator as much as to his loyalty that he not only survived the war but prospered under both regimes. It was Morton in fact who arranged Henry's marriage to Elizabeth of York, which united both houses under one kingship and brought an end to the Wars of the Roses.

Morton, knowledgeable in both Roman canon law and English common law, was one of the last prelates to become a high-ranking official in both Church and state. The Reformation of 1517 began a process that altered the extent of ecclesiastical involvement in secular government, a practice that had its origins in the early fourth century when Constantine utilized Christianity as a means of unifying the vast Roman Empire. During the early fifth century, the western half of the Roman Empire crumbled amidst barbarian invasions and civil disorder, and Church officials helped to fill the leadership vacuum that resulted from the collapse of Roman civil authority. As the feudal system developed during the Early Middle Ages (c. 476–c. 1000), bishops and abbots often assumed responsibility in the affairs of local governments, and popes, cardinals, and bishops regularly governed alongside kings and lords, sometimes contesting their power. All of this began to change after 1517 when local governments in northern Germany widely rejected Church intervention in civil affairs. In England, Cardinal Thomas Wolsey (like Morton, another churchman of outstanding ability) became lord chancellor in 1515, but he was replaced in 1529 by a layman, Sir Thomas More, and from then on, no cleric would ever again be appointed to the lord chancellorship. The ultimate repudiation of ecclesiastical authority, however, was reserved to Henry VIII, who coerced Parliament in 1534 into proclaiming him "Supreme Head of the Church of England," thus displacing the pope within his realm in the spiritual sphere as well as the secular.

These events were in the not-too-distant future from "Young More's" tenure as a page in Archbishop Morton's household at Lambeth Palace where he associated with sons of high-ranking nobles, and to have received such a privilege indicates the respect his father, John More, enjoyed among England's elite. Morton was also a patron of what we today know as "Renaissance humanism," and in addition to a formation in etiquette and social graces, he provided the boys in his service with an outstanding scholarly education and introduction to Renaissance culture. When Morton realized that More would be better served by moving on, he arranged for him to be enrolled at his alma mater, Canterbury

College in Oxford. Morton was elevated to the cardinalate sometime after 1492 and died eight years later.

More remained at Oxford for two difficult but profitable years. He was often without money, as his father kept him on such a tight budget that Thomas could not afford to repair his shoes. Nor did he earn a degree, and there is no record of the courses he took or if Morton or his father expected him to pursue a career in the Church or as a secular lawyer. Canterbury was a Benedictine college that offered an education in canon and civil law as well as other traditional liberal arts courses such as logic, grammar, rhetoric, and philosophy.[18] Thomas would have listened to public disputations and practiced his exceptional oratory skills in which he had shown marked ability at Saint Anthony's School and Lambeth Palace, and most importantly, he would have refined his Latin conversational skills. It is worth noting that More was studying at Canterbury College while Thomas Wolsey, five years More's senior, was not far away in residence at Magdalen College.

More was fifteen years old in 1493 when his father withdrew him from Canterbury College and brought him back to London to study English common law at New Inn, one of the ten or so Inns of Chancery. Prior to the Norman invasion in 1066, the prevailing law in England was Anglo-Saxon law, which resembled the law of the northern Germanic tribes on the continent. After

---

[18] The seven classic liberal arts of a liberal arts curriculum at this time included the trivium (grammar, logic, and rhetoric) and the quadrivium (astronomy, geometry, mathematics, and music).

Duke William of Normandy's victory over the Anglo-Saxon king, Harold Godwinson, he became King of England and distributed much of the land to the Norman nobles who fought for him at the Battle of Hastings. These nobles replaced the former Anglo-Saxon landowners as feudal lords bringing with them their own customary law which, over time, coalesced with Anglo-Saxon law. As the foreign ruler of a generally discontented people, William I sought to centralize his power and quell unrest by emphasizing royal prerogative and enforcing the king's judicial authority. This concentration of royal power required the development of a bureaucracy and eventually promoted a national sentiment more quickly in England than anywhere else in Europe. By 1300, England had a popular and legitimate monarchy assisted by the early stages of Parliament. King William and his royal successors remained the Dukes of Normandy, allowing them to draw income from the Duchy of Normandy and providing them with a reserve of loyal Norman knights. These resources made it possible (and tempting) for the King of England to acquire additional feudal territories in France—a state of affairs that contributed to the perpetuation of the Hundred Years' War.

The development of English common law as a confluence of Anglo-Saxon law and Norman law was a gradual and incremental process that occurred over centuries and consisted of a lengthy series of small decisions made by individual lawyers and judges. It is not clear, however, what influence ecclesiastical law had on its development. One opinion among scholars is that a reciprocal but limited influence existed between the two, and that canon law, which had been developing for centuries on the continent, served as a source from which common lawyers could draw. Canon law had become universal throughout Europe during the High Middle Ages and was the only international code of law. It was practiced in the English church courts, which existed alongside the king's courts, and overlapping responsibilities inevitably developed as both laws evolved. This often resulted in disagreements (and at times, a rivalry) between ecclesiastical courts and royal courts over rights and jurisdiction, as well as disputes over ancient privileges.

Lawyers in both courts may have borrowed ideas and arguments from each other, since we know that English common lawyers often used Latin maxims found in canon law texts. Legal codes are not static entities but evolve and adapt over time according to social, economic, and political realities, and canon law during the High Middle Ages was often adapted to local custom throughout Europe as much as it depended on the texts of the Decretals. On the other hand, some scholars hold that Roman canon law did not have the same impact in England during the High Middle Ages as it did on the continent because the legal system in England became more efficient and centralized at an earlier stage than in other parts of Europe, and the principles of ecclesiastical law and canon law texts were of little or no use in the English secular courts. Even if one accepts the argument for reciprocal influence, it is certain that many areas of English common law could not be adapted to ecclesiastical law, and the influence that one legal system had on another may have been so negligible that they were, in practice, mutually exclusive legal systems.

In any case, there is clear evidence during the reign of King Edward I (r. 1272–1307) of a class of professional civil lawyers who undertook a period of specialized training and were governed by a code of conduct that included penal sanctions for unethical behavior, and records show they practiced in secular and royal courts. The elite of this class were the serjeants-at-law and the judges who presided in the royal courts. Scholars today note how different the English common law courts were from the ecclesiastical courts: (a) common lawyers and judges were trained separately from their church counterparts and in a dissimilar system of law; (b) their sets of procedures were different, as were their competencies and legal rules; and (c) they spoke different languages—English and Anglo-Norman French (Law French) in common law courts, and Latin in ecclesiastical courts. There were, however, lawyers and judges who were trained in both systems, some of whom were ordained, and proficiency of this kind was highly prized by those aspiring to royal service.

It is important for us to realize here that the dichotomy which exists in the modern world between *laws proper to religion* and *laws proper to the state* did not exist in the late medieval world. Law in its most general sense may be viewed as a codification of morals and ethics, but to the late medieval mind, all law reflected and participated in divine law. The medieval world certainly distinguished between the "spiritual sword" of religious authority and the "temporal sword" of secular authority, but the conflict between the two had not yet been satisfactorily resolved and the modern notion of "separation between Church and state" simply did not exist in the pre-Reformation mind. The medieval jurist held that the laws of God (*leges Dei*) and laws promulgated by human legislators (e.g., kings, parliaments) share a common source in God, even if some laws are directly attributable to God (e.g., the Decalogue, Gospel precepts) and others less so (e.g., property law, inheritance law). In the medieval mindset, human laws were believed to have a divine origin, and English common law was understood to be grounded in both reason and the law of God.[19]

This general principle which formed the basis of legal systems in the medieval world—that *all legislative power comes from God* — and the belief that religion, law, and government were inseparably intertwined were key factors in the clash between Henry VIII and Pope Clement VII. Thomas More became entangled in this dispute only at Henry's insistence, and despite resigning from royal service and his intention to remain publicly silent, he was unable to remove himself entirely from it. In the end, he was forced to choose between pope and king.

The notion of the indivisibility and divine origin of religion, law, and government is also key in understanding More's unwavering opposition to Luther and the other reformers. He

---

[19] Perhaps this understanding was inspired by Romans 13:1–7.

viewed Luther's attack on the pope and Henry VIII as an attack on the established social order and time-honored tradition. As a humanist scholar, More supported constructive reform within the Church and society, but he believed that individual leaders and governing institutions could not be easily discarded without creating anarchy and disorder, even if human authority is an imperfect manifestation of God's authority. In this sense, More would have agreed with the spiritual maxim that *all rebellion leads to death.*

~

Thomas More remained at New Inn in London for two years. Like the other Inns of Chancery, New Inn offered a pre-law program that prepared its students for advanced legal studies in one of the four Inns of Court. Upon graduation, Thomas entered nearby Lincoln's Inn where his father was a member. He was eighteen years old and the coursework offered at Lincoln's Inn normally lasted from four to eight years depending on the individual student's ability. More remained at Lincoln's Inn from 1496 until he graduated in 1502.

8

Formation and Community
A Fellowship of Christian Humanists

Students of Lincoln's Inn were required to take classes for half of the year, a schedule which gave them time to pursue other interests. More had acquired a taste for intellectual study and spiritual development at a young age and maintained a regime throughout his life of rising early in the morning for reading, writing, and quiet meditation, even during those years when he was occupied with professional commitments and the duties of royal service. During his six years at Lincoln's Inn, More was also able to establish formative relationships with older men who were also exceptional scholars, some of whom were clerics, which served to supplement the formal education he was receiving at Lincoln's Inn. This group of English Christian humanists later became known as the "London Reformers" and included:

- John Colet (1467–1519), who attended Saint Anthony's School before studying at Cambridge and Oxford. He then traveled to Italy where he experienced an increase in religious fervor. Upon his return to England, he was ordained a priest and, amidst his other duties, served as More's confessor and spiritual advisor. He later founded Saint Paul's School in London and served as its dean.

- William Lily (1468–1522), a grammarian, studied at Oxford before traveling to Jerusalem, Greece, and Italy. When he returned to London, he tutored in Greek and Latin and wrote a popular Latin grammar book that was used into the nineteenth century. Thomas More studied privately with Lily, and they became close friends. Among Lily's other distinctions, John Colet appointed him as Saint Paul's first high master.

- Thomas Linacre (1460–1524), who studied Greek with William de Selling at Oxford before traveling to Florence, Padua, and Rome, where he continued his studies in Greek and Latin. He developed an interest in medicine while in Italy and earned a medical degree at the University of Padua. He then returned to England to practice medicine and teach Greek (one of his students was Thomas More). Henry VII appointed Linacre to be a tutor to Prince Arthur, and he later became Henry VIII's physician.

- William Grocyn (1446–1519), who studied at Oxford and later held academic posts there as fellow and reader. In his early forties, he traveled to Italy and was permitted by Lorenzo de Medici to study Greek with the tutors of Lorenzo's children. He returned to Oxford to teach Greek studies and later served as the warden of All Saints College.

These English scholars were part of a growing international community of humanists who were engaged in a process of educational reform, or "rebirth," in keeping with the spirit of the times (what we know today as the Renaissance). This educational reform movement was to some extent a reaction against scholastic obscurantism and overspeculation. Scholasticism, with its divisions, parts, and lists, had been the dominant educational model in Christendom for more than three centuries, and great churchmen like Saints Anselm and Thomas Aquinas developed it as both a method of education and a system of philosophy and theology to instill intellectual credibility into religious doctrine. But Scholasticism was also employed in theological speculations that sometimes ventured into the absurd (e.g., Could Christ have been incarnated as a mule, and if so, can a mule be crucified?). Humanists, many of whom were reared in scholastic methodology, derided such impractical speculation and in its place offered what came to be known as the "New Learning"—a term later adopted by Catholics in the sixteenth century and used pejoratively to disparage Protestant theology.

The humanist program was to some extent a reaction against Scholasticism, but men like Thomas More would have recoiled at the notion that it was revolutionary. The humanist project for them involved the *rediscovery* of insights found in the writings of ancient pagan authors—not truly new, but timeless and merely forgotten during the "medium aevum," or "middle age," and now reemerging (rebirth, reawakening) into the intellectual conscious-ness of their day. Humanists viewed the errors of Scholasticism in the same way they regarded the clerical abuses for which the Church was universally blamed (simony, pluralism, avarice, absenteeism, etc.), but their attempt at reform through a program of classical learning was not intended to be a revolt against Church authority or doctrine. Amendment of institutional faults need not result in rebellion, and most of the early humanists were loyal churchmen and devout Christians who advocated constructive reform rather than revolution or division. This helps to explain why men like Thomas More were sensitive to allegations that the New Learning had fostered Protestantism.

But humanism had in fact been instrumental in the rise and growth of Protestantism. The emphasis placed on pagan classical studies as a companion to theology and the shift in focus from divinity to humanity had important if unintended consequences, namely that it encouraged critical thinking and individual interpretation which led to the questioning of authority and doctrine. Scholars learned in Hebrew and Greek began to study the Bible in its original languages and published new translations, some of which were in the vernacular. Since all translations are interpretations, disagreement arose over word choice and accuracy. Further, reformers like Luther lamented that many of the Church's doctrines and practices could not be found in the Bible. The early humanists did not seek to topple the established order, but the educational reform they advocated took unforeseen turns.

~

Christian humanists like Thomas More and the other London Reformers did not wish to begin a social and religious revolution but believed instead that "honorable studies" and "sound learning" promote intelligent and responsible citizenship that leads to the perfection of society. In a word, Christian humanists sought *virtue—moral, intellectual, civic,* and *social virtue.* They strove to "live well" in Saint Augustine's "City of Man" (human civilization in this temporal age as distinct from the eternal "City of God"), which requires the practice of moral, intellectual, civic, and social virtue.

~

The Church has perpetually taught that there is no greater virtue than *charity* (the love of God and neighbor), and Thomas More conscientiously practiced charity throughout his life. Among his many good deeds, he regularly visited the poor to give alms, and when his duties prevented this, he had family members go in his place. He also invited the poor to his table and gave them gifts, and in the winter of 1528 during a famine, he fed one hundred people a day at his home. When his farm was severely damaged by fire in 1529, More refused to dismiss any of his workers until they found new jobs. His devotion to God included faithful church attendance, and he found time amidst his many responsibilities to sing in the choir and participate in public processions.

He was generous to his family as well, often giving coins to his children, and he was one of the first to support the education of women by giving his daughters an education equal to what English sons received. The generosity he showed to others, however, was not accompanied by any taint of self-indulgence. Whatever the modern world may think of medieval penitential customs, he practiced corporal austerity by wearing a hair shirt from early adulthood until death as a means of subduing his sensual appetite and bridling his concupiscence, and as he got older, he became notably abstemious with food and drink.

Thomas More's prayer seems to have been effective as well. In 1528, his daughter Margaret was deathly ill with "sweating sickness" and the doctors could find no effective remedy. More retired to his "New Building" to pray for her and received an intuition to give her an enema which, once administered, alleviated her symptoms and restored her to health. He also prayed for the conversion of his son-in-law, William Roper, who would have been severely punished by Cardinal Wolsey for becoming a Lutheran had he not been More's son-in-law. In due time, Roper returned to Catholicism after becoming disenchanted with the fragmentation of the reform movement and the disparate teaching of its numerous leaders.

It is safe to believe that More's prayer life was efficacious because it was rooted in charity—the queen of all of the virtues. Evidence of his charitable disposition can be found in the accounts left by Erasmus and his early biographers, which depict him as generous, kind, affable, and good-natured to everyone. Even at his trial for treason, he treated his accusers and judges as if they were his friends and sincerely wished they were. Erasmus knew More from 1499 until More's execution in 1535 and wrote that he "never showed ill intent to anyone."

9

Formation in Life and Holiness
Thomas More's True Vocation

We do not know what John More thought about Thomas' discernment to the priesthood and religious life, but we know that from about 1501 to 1504, Thomas spent time at the Charterhouse in London living and praying with Carthusian monks. The monastery was not far from Lincoln's Inn or his family home, and it was disbanded during the Dissolution of the Monasteries (1536–1541) after its prior, John Houghton (1486–1535), was hanged, drawn, and quartered at Tyburn for refusing to consent to the Act of Supremacy. Remnants of the London Charterhouse still survive today.

We also do not know if More stayed in the guest quarters of the monastery during those times when he was not in residence at Lincoln's Inn or if he acquired external temporary lodging near the monastery, but early chroniclers record that he lived devoutly with the monks for about four years. He may have risen with them in the middle of the night to chant Matins and Lauds in the cold and stillness of the monastery church and then attended the other hours of the Divine Office that were sung during the day in common: Prime, Terce, Sext, None, Vespers, and Compline. He may have been given manual labor to occupy his time between the hours of prayer, perhaps working in a garden or helping to prepare food in the kitchen. Or he may have been privileged to spend time in the scriptorium where monks laboriously copied manuscripts by hand, a traditional monastic occupation but one the printing press made obsolete. He probably fasted with the monks and enjoyed the silence, solitude, and contemplation that is the charism of the Carthusian Order. One of More's early biographers records that he considered becoming a priest, but he never took vows and after four years of vocational discernment, he decided that his true vocation was to marriage and family and service to society in the legal profession. He may have also realized at this time, or perhaps in later years, that his vocation also included service through scholarship and literary endeavors.

The few years More resided with the Carthusians in London provided him with a spiritual formation that complemented the intellectual and professional formation he received in formal studies. Even during the busiest times of his life when he was a family man, property owner, lawyer, judge, civil servant, and royal servant, he remained faithful to his habit of rising early in the morning for prayer and study. Later in life, he had constructed a "New Building" on his property in Chelsea that included a chapel, library, and study. Every morning, he rose early as he had done for many years to retire to the silence and solitude of his own retreat house where he cultivated those virtues necessary for his vocation in life.

Thomas More was indeed a man of lifelong formation—*spiritual, intellectual, human,* and *professional*—as much as he was a man of virtue—*moral, intellectual, civic,* and *social.* Formation in all of these areas of life is an essential aspect of character development and of acquiring a conscience that can properly distinguish between true goods and specious goods. The cultivation of virtue is not an easy task, nor is it a job to be done once. Becoming a saint, and especially a hero-saint, requires formation, sacrifice, dedication, and the commitment to persevere even during the most difficult of times.

Yet every human life is unique and unrepeatable and there is not one formation program that is suitable for all, even if there are common characteristics between one life and another and shared formation activities in which all persons must engage (e.g., prayer, sacrifice, the practice of virtue). The individuality of human life and the differences between individual persons and their Sacred Concerns (see Book One of this series) require that God have a unique formation plan specific to each person. Joan of Arc's path to hero-sainthood, for example, was very dissimilar to Thomas More's. What is paramount is God's will and the recognition that he has an individual plan for each of us. God is the ultimate Formation Director and he will form us to complete our particular mission and vocation on earth as well as sanctify and purify us in preparation for heaven—if we only cooperate with his grace. Our primary task then, and one common to all, is to *listen* and *obey*. This is of the highest priority in Christian discipleship and service to God. Thomas More spent those early hours of the morning reading and listening in prayer and reflection to God's still, small voice (1 Kings 19:12) which he then obeyed. All Christian formation ultimately leads to holiness, and obedience to the will of God is the essence of holiness.

Thomas More was a man of lifelong formation, and when it came time to die, he died well. Unlike most of his contemporaries who were presented with the same choice pressed upon him, More chose the narrow path that led to martyrdom. People who work with the dying in hospice care say, "People die as they lived." Thomas More lived a life of formation and was a man of virtue and service, and he died like one—a servant of God and neighbor, even when that neighbor was a king who unjustly sought his life.

10

Rise of the Minister
Career and Family

The years between 1501 and 1504 when Thomas More was discerning his vocation at the London Charterhouse were not dedicated entirely to law school and contemplative activities, and once he graduated from Lincoln's Inn in 1502, he became more involved in the social world and legal affairs of London. He was invited to lecture on Saint Augustine's *The City of God* at Saint Lawrence Jewry in 1501, and between 1503 and 1506, he served as a reader (lecturer) in Law at Furnival's Inn, an Inn of Chancery. Also noteworthy was that he began studying Greek with Thomas Linacre in 1501. Once he had discerned his true vocation to marriage, family, and the legal profession, he ceased frequenting the London Charterhouse in 1504 to devote himself more fully to his career as a common lawyer and seeking a suitable spouse.

In his biography of More, William Roper wrote that his father-in-law was elected to the House of Commons in 1504 and incurred Henry VII's wrath by opposing the king's request for a grant of taxation, but it seems out of character for More to oppose the king's will so publicly and no other source confirms this, so it is unlikely to have occurred. It is certain, however, that he was elected financial secretary of Lincoln's Inn in 1507, and in December 1509—with the help of the powerful Mercers' Guild who had previously admitted him as a member—he was elected to Parliament. In 1510, More became one of the two undersheriffs of London in which capacity he provided legal advice to the mayor and sheriff and served as a judge in the sheriff's court. His reputation and rise to prominence during this period before his entrance into royal service in 1518 was confirmed in 1515 when the king's council, because of his expertise in commercial law, requested that he assist in a delegation to Bruges and Antwerp sent to renegotiate diplomatic and mercantile treaties (most notably involving the wool trade) between England and Flanders. The mission was so successful that King Henry VIII offered him an annual pension which he declined, possibly because it would have obliged him to royal service and thus created a conflict of interest with More's private law practice, his employment as a city administrator, and his involvement in the politics of London. In 1516, More joined his father, John More, as a member of the prestigious Star Chamber under the direction of Cardinal Wolsey, who in 1515 had become Lord Chancellor of England. In 1517, More was appointed to a diplomatic mission to Calais to negotiate mercantile disputes between England and France. It was also in 1517 that Luther posted his *Ninety-five Theses*.

In addition to his duties as a lawyer, judge, public administrator, and diplomat, More continued his literary pursuits, much of it in the early hours of the morning. He had been writing poetry since 1496, and in 1510, he published *The Life of John Picus, Earl of Mirandola*, a partially translated and partially composed biography written in English about a Florentine humanist and layman. Between 1513 and 1518, he worked on an unfinished and unpublished manuscript entitled *The History of King Richard III*, which was meant to buttress the Tudor regime, encourage Henry VIII toward a humanist vision of Christian kingship, and warn him against the temptation to tyranny. In 1516, he published his most celebrated work, *Utopia*, a treatise written in the style of travel literature that became popular during the early sixteenth century in the wake of the discoveries made by European explorers beginning in 1492.[20] In *Utopia* (Gr. "nowhere"), More gives an account of an island nation composed of city-states that was governed by an elective monarchy but prohibited a hereditary aristocracy. More's *Utopia* has been compared to Plato's *Republic*, but *Utopia* was written primarily as a critique of European society and a polemic against privileged wealth rather than to describe an ideal state, as was Plato's *Republic*. After the beginning of the Protestant Reformation in 1517, More used his literary skills to compose refutations of Luther and the other reformers.

At the end of 1517 or early 1518, More left his position on the Star Chamber to join the king's court as a councilor attendant and member of the Privy Chamber. He had been initially unwilling to enter royal service because it required him to sacrifice his private

---

[20] Known as the Age of Discovery, or the Age of Exploration.

law practice and his involvement in the politics of London. It also meant that he would have less time for his family to whom he was very devoted.

In 1504, More proposed marriage to Jane Colt (1488–1511), the eldest daughter of John Colt of Essex, and they were wed in 1505. She bore him Margaret that same year, Elizabeth in 1506, Cecily in 1507, and John in 1509. Jane died in 1511 at the age of twenty-three, possibly during childbirth or from illness, but More obtained a dispensation to remarry quickly and wed Alice Middleton (1474–1551) within a month of Jane's death. Alice, almost four years older than More and fourteen years older than his previous wife, was the widow of a London silk merchant to whom she bore a daughter. She was also a property owner from her previous marriage. More sought to wed Alice so quickly because she was a respectable woman in English society and he had young children to raise and a household to maintain as well as a career to cultivate. He never professed a physical or romantic attraction to her, which some biographers speculate was another reason he married her. More was concerned throughout his life to practice virtue and Alice posed no temptation to him against chastity. She bore him no children during the twenty-four years they were married, and judging from his comments, the marriage was less than ideal. But despite what appears to be a mutual lack of satisfaction, Alice More was a dependable housekeeper and property manager, and she remained faithful to him until his execution in 1535.

11

Erasmus of Rotterdam
Friendship and the Love of Learning

Thomas More first met the Dutch Renaissance scholar Erasmus of Rotterdam in 1499, and they soon became close friends, regularly exchanging letters across the English Channel. Erasmus visited More after his marriage to Jane Colt in 1505, and probably at Erasmus's urging, More made his first trip to the continent around 1508 to visit the universities in Paris and Louvain. Erasmus had spent a few years at the University of Louvain and had contacts at the University of Paris, and although no record survives to confirm this, it is supposed that he arranged for More to meet some of his academic associates. More later said that he was primarily interested in learning about the curricula and teaching methods that were being employed at these renowned institutions of learning.

More's trip to Louvain and Paris reveals another important aspect of his character: He was more than a distinguished scholar and lover of books; he was an *educator* at heart—interested in improving course content and implementing the new pedagogical methods that were being advanced during the early sixteenth century. In fact, humanists as a group were avid enthusiasts for developing educational theory, and scholars like More sought to apply theoretical knowledge to practice. It is likely he would have found fulfillment in life as a university lecturer in law or perhaps as a teacher in a liberal arts curriculum. In addition to the teaching and lecturing posts he held before entering royal service in 1518, he taught grammar at Oxford at the same time Erasmus was teaching Greek at Cambridge. His love for education was also evident in his conduct at home. After marrying seventeen-year-old Jane Colt in 1505, he attempted to give her the education she had not received in her youth. In the rearing of his children, he structured his home as if it were a school and implemented a humanist model of education—what he and other humanists called a "renaissance of good letters"—by designing a curriculum that included courses in history, philosophy, theology, language, literature, math, and science, and hiring tutors from Oxford and Cambridge to instruct the students. His home school eventually grew to serve around a dozen youths and offered a quality education that rivaled London's finest schools.

While More was in accord with the spirit of his times regarding humanist education models, he was well ahead of his contemporaries in the education of women. He instructed his daughters using the same classical curriculum he provided to his son and his other male students, and his female students received an education comparable to that afforded only to princesses of royal families. In his highly influential *Utopia*, More endorsed the education of women and their value in the workplace, and Erasmus later admitted that More had convinced him of the importance of educating women.

While Thomas sought to instill in the youths in his charge a *love of learning*, he recognized that this was secondary to nurturing in them a *desire for God*—and if his home was modeled on a school, then it was also modeled on a monastery. More understood that intellectual formation gained from academic study is only one aspect of an overall formation program, and that a proper Christian formation must address the spiritual and religious dimension of the human person as well. Toward this end, he passed on the fruits of his own spiritual formation, particularly what he learned at the London Charterhouse. Thomas knew that God must be first in all things, and perhaps the greatest lesson he ever imparted during his time on earth was that he laid down his life for this truth.

12

The New King, Henry VIII

Life was ebbing away from Henry VII in April 1509, but he died knowing that the Tudor line of succession was secure. He had ruled England since his victory over Richard III at the Battle of Bosworth Field in 1485, and by marrying Elizabeth, daughter of the Yorkist king, Edward IV, he united the Houses of York and Lancaster and put an end to the Wars of the Roses. Except for one brief uprising in 1487 that supported Lambert Simnel (a Yorkist aspirant), Henry's rule was refreshingly peaceful. The battles fought between 1455 and 1485 had thinned the ranks of the nobility and many of the old families had died out. In their place, new nobility arose loyal only to Henry. For his part, the king was an efficient administrator (even if his fiscal policies and taxation schemes were unpopular), and he brought much-needed stability to the realm by solidifying the authority of the monarchy and reducing the power of the nobility. This created the conditions for an increase in trade and the growth of a prosperous middle class, and England's economy flourished. What remained of the medieval way of life with its regional tyrants of noble birth was steadily passing into history during Henry VII's reign, and England was developing rapidly into a nation-state whose political center was a powerful monarchy.

Henry VII outlived his first son, Arthur (1486–1502), and his wife, Elizabeth (1466–1503), before passing away in 1509. His second son, Henry, was eleven years old when he became heir and seventeen when he ascended the throne as Henry VIII. Prince Arthur had been married to Catherine of Aragon (1485–1536) for only a few months before his untimely death, and Henry VIII, after having obtained the necessary dispensation from Pope Julius II, married her shortly after his accession. Queen Catherine, however, was unable to provide Henry with a male heir during their twenty-four years of marriage, and in the wake of the dynastic struggles that preceded his father's reign, and because of the priority the king placed on a peaceful transition of power, Henry deemed this failure intolerable. Despite the papal dispensation that permitted him to marry Catherine, he would one day seek to have his marriage annulled so that he might marry again, but the pope would not grant it. Confident in his abilities and as obstinate and self-willed as he was tall, robust, and physically powerful, Henry determined that nature's denial and the pope's refusal should not prevent him from obtaining a male heir.

But these events could not be foreseen in 1509, and the genial, vigorous young king rose to power amidst great expectation, as if his coronation heralded the dawn of a new era. Henry VII's taxation policies were widely unpopular among his subjects, and the new king and his ministers quickly removed them. Yet the deceased king had been a patron of Renaissance learning and raised his sons with tutors, books, and piety, and humanists in England and on the continent rejoiced when Henry VIII succeeded to the throne. Erasmus, one of the most important scholars of his day, was moved to return to England in 1509 to receive Henry's generous patronage.[21] The humanist preoccupation with peace as a necessary precondition for reform, social prosperity, and the advancement of learning, however, would eventually clash with the king's infatuation with chivalric ideals and medieval wars of conquest that later motivated him to disturb the peace of France.

And there were other disturbing aspects of Henry VIII's character that were incongruent with humanist goals and would emerge in subsequent years. It will suffice in this brief sketch to shed light on his character by deferring to the words of two men who knew him well and served him as lord chancellor—Thomas Wolsey and Thomas More. Wolsey once counseled another royal servant, "I warn you to be well advised and assured what matter you put into his head; for you shall never pull it out again." And when referring to the self-will and rashness of the king, Wolsey stated, "Rather than he will either miss or want any part of his will or appetite, he will put the loss of one half of his realm in danger."

---

[21] Erasmus began teaching Greek at Cambridge in 1511 and stayed in England until 1514.

Thomas More, having received a personal visit from Henry at More's home in Chelsea, during which the king put his arm around him and spoke to him as if to a close friend, later said to his son-in-law, William Roper, "If my head could win him a castle in France … it should not fail to go." He later advised Thomas Cromwell, who became Henry's chief minister after More was executed in 1535, "Ever tell him what he ought to do, but never tell him what he is able to do… For if a lion knew his own strength, hard were it for any man to rule him."

13

Life Journey and Formation
The Road to Royal Service

Thomas More was forty years old when he accepted Henry VIII's invitation to enter royal service. He could hardly have done otherwise and remained faithful to all that he held most dear. More was at heart a true Englishman and a man of *law, order, duty,* and *tradition*—all of which England was amply blessed with.[22] More was also a man of *community*, and the many communities to which he belonged included: (a) the domestic community of his family; (b) the community of citizens in his hometown of London; (c) the Church as a community of Christian believers; (d) the kingdom of England as a community of royal subjects; (e) the English humanists as a community of scholars and circle of friends; (f) the international community of Christian humanists throughout Europe; and although he did not pursue a monastic

---

[22] *Duty*, among other things, requires obedience to legitimate authority, a trait which More valued throughout his life and first displayed in the filial obedience he showed to his father. Obedience to the king was a logical and necessary consequence of More's deeply held sense of duty.

vocation, he nevertheless spent nearly four formative years associating with (g) the religious community of Carthusian monks at the priory in London.

More recognized that *law, order, duty, tradition,* and a sense of *community* were essential for the proper maintenance and functioning of society and the only guarantee against anarchy. He also understood that responsible participation as a member of any community requires the practice of *virtue—moral, intellectual, civic,* and *social.* The Christian practice of virtue implies a call to service and obedience, and for Thomas More, this ultimately meant obedience to the pope and king. In the end, Henry VIII would force him to choose between the two, and More's decision—and there was never ambiguity in his mind as to his priorities—would lead to his martyrdom on Tower Hill.

But Thomas was aware of the dangers of royal service before he accepted Henry's invitation, just as he was aware of the potential consequences of refusing to submit to the king's will over the pope's. His decisions were always well-informed, since he was before all else, a man of *prayer, study, reflection,* and *formation* who searched for truth and light in all its forms. The *human, intellectual, spiritual,* and *professional formation* he received from academic study, private intellectual pursuits, and his prayer life prepared him well for the important decisions he was required to make. In particular, the education that common lawyers received in England at this time rivaled the education imparted to high-ranking clergymen, and as a group, common lawyers were the most educated class of laymen in England. Sir John Fortescue (1394–1479), a former Chief Justice of the King's Bench, wrote an influential treatise on English common law in which he argued that all justice flows from God and that there is a similarity between the law of the Church and the law of the land, which implies a similarity between priests and lawyers. Lawyers as educated professionals administer the law of the land and are in some respects akin to priests who minister within the Church, and according to Fortescue, common lawyers must be shown deference in matters of secular law just as priests are shown deference in matters of religion and canon law. Fortescue's theory no doubt fueled the rivalry that was intensifying in England between the ecclesiastical and lay courts, but it also fostered the notion that lawyers are *ministers* of secular law in a manner analogous to priests who are ministers in the Church. This was certainly how More viewed himself—as a minister of the common law and a servant of justice—and unlike many other civil lawyers and judges of his time, he practiced assiduous virtue.[23]

More's education extended beyond professional knowledge, however, and after years of private study, writing, and publishing, he became one of the leading humanist scholars of his day. Even so, it was no small matter to enter royal service to Henry VIII, and More was familiar from the outset with the king's dispositions and

---

[23] During his years in private practice, civil service, and royal service, More acquired the reputation of being utterly incorruptible.

habits of mind.[24] He had known Henry for almost twenty years, having first met him in the summer of 1499 at Eltham Palace, Prince Henry's home when he was the Duke of York. Prince Arthur, the Duke of Wales, was still alive then, but the health and vigor of body and constitution that nature bestowed on Henry was not granted in fair proportion to his older sibling, and Arthur died prematurely in 1502. Erasmus was present at this first meeting in 1499, and he, More, and the other European humanists were brimming with enthusiasm when Henry ascended the throne ten years later.

But by 1518, the honeymoon was over and the initial fervor had subsided. Henry's military ventures in France and his determination for *potestas* and *imperium* in England as well as his desire for influence in the political affairs on the continent contrasted sharply with the humanist belief that peace was the prerequisite for unity and their dream of a universal brotherhood of rulers within Christendom. In Henry VIII, the humanists had hoped for a Renaissance monarch and philosopher king (the ideal ruler in Plato's *Republic*) who would abandon the medieval penchant for war and conquest and advance their program of reform in education and society. But Henry VIII had his own vision of kingship and understanding of royal prerogative that in later years would become deep-seated, self-righteous conviction.

---

[24] More and those closest to him were aware of Henry's interest in chivalry and admiration for the heroic deeds performed by his royal predecessors, particularly Henry V.

Henry was twenty-seven years old in 1518 when Thomas More entered royal service. He was at the height of his physical powers, and like other English monarchs before him, desired glory through martial conquest and the acquisition of possessions on the continent, particularly in France. This would provide a significant challenge to More and his humanist convictions, but in addition to being a man of *prayer, study, reflection*, and *formation*, he was also a man of *discernment*, and he must have approached this decision with the same circumspection he used when he discerned his vocation to marriage and family and career as a common lawyer.

Basic Rules of Discernment:
1. Pray and reflect
2. Take your time
3. Seek counsel
4. If necessary, fast and abstain.

There is no record of the length or quality of More's discernment, but with respect to the content of this series, we might wonder if he felt *predestined* for royal service, that it was a part of a divine calling (*vocation*), and that he had been chosen and prepared for it from birth (*mission*). Perhaps he got a sense that his rise in English society was part of a divinely ordained *mission sequence*, the next logical step of which was service to the king, and perhaps he recognized the king's invitation as a *kairos moment*— an opportunity presented once in time and eternity that requires a decision before it passes away never to return. And perhaps he felt at peace when he decided to accept Henry's invitation, even if he was aware of the potentially fatal consequences that such acceptance might entail.

It is a principle in the spiritual life that one must give up something to get something, and if the character of a person can be measured by what he or she is willing to sacrifice for what he or she most values, then it can also be said that one's character can be measured by one's willingness to accept a potential, future sacrifice in order to do what one feels called by God to do in the present moment. In Thomas More's case, that potential sacrifice became actual, and in return for his willingness to sacrifice his life, he received the fulfillment of his mission on earth and the eternal honor of martyrdom and hero-sainthood.

~

When Thomas More entered royal service in 1518, Henry VIII told him that he expected him to be the king's loyal servant, but God's first. It is not likely that this admonition gave More a false sense of security that Henry had his priorities in order, but it came from a man who probably wished it at the time and was received by a man who had already intended to do precisely as he was being advised. The medieval notion that kings ruled by divine right still prevailed at the beginning of the sixteenth century, and More believed, as did many of his contemporaries, that monarchy was a divinely ordained institution. More viewed it as a Christian duty to serve God, and as an English subject, a duty to serve the king (who was not at this time the selfish and violent despot he would later become). And More must have felt an additional obligation to accept an appointment as a royal counselor *because* he was a humanist scholar.[25] Humanists as a group desired influence over rulers so that they might have their ideas implemented in government policy, but few ever attained a position close enough to a monarch to provide direct counsel. Most humanists would have envied the privilege of proximity to a monarch that More was being offered, since ideas are more powerful when recommended by a trusted counselor.

~

It is noteworthy that Thomas More began his career as a royal servant at about the same time that Martin Luther began his career as a Protestant reformer. It is also noteworthy that these two men shared similar but divergent pasts. Luther's father, Hans Luther, insisted that his son become a lawyer so that he might rise to prominence in German society, but Martin disobeyed his father and withdrew from law school to become an Augustinian monk. Thomas More's father, John (German, "Hans"), also wanted his son to become a lawyer, and although Thomas discerned a Carthusian vocation for four years, he graduated from law school and chose law as a profession. Both men rose to prominence beyond their fathers' expectations and both became famous figures in history.

---

[25] Even if the term "humanist" was not in use at this time.

Luther posted his *Ninety-five Theses* on October 31, 1517—less than a year before More entered royal service—but it is unlikely that More considered this event as anything unusual, if he were even aware of it. Public scholarly debate was a normal pastime of medieval academic life, and even the pope initially viewed it as a "squabble among monks." Nor could More have foreseen the implications of Luther's posting. Their paths diverged early in life over the choice of a career, and they would diverge again over religious conviction. Luther would eventually reject the pope and the established Church, while More would oppose Luther and the other reformers as being against all that he held most dear—law, order, duty, tradition, community, and virtue. They never met in person, but their disagreements put them on a collision course that erupted in the polemical tracts they wrote and published against each other.

In 1520, Luther published *On the Babylonian Captivity of the Church* in which he denounced four of the seven sacraments, affirming only baptism, penance, and the Eucharist. Henry VIII responded by publishing *Defense of the Seven Sacraments* in 1521, for which he was awarded the title "Defender of the Faith" by Pope Leo X. Luther countered with *Against Henry, King of the English* (1522), which was little more than a crude, personal attack that contained almost no theological argument. The king would not condescend to reply to this invective, but asked More to do it for him, and in 1523, More published *Response to Luther* under the pseudonym William Ross (not without some vulgarity and less-than-saintly rhetoric of his own).

14

The Fullness of Time
Royal Service (1518 to 1529)

More resigned the office of Undersheriff of London in July 1518 and became the king's Master of Requests that same year. In June 1520, he aided in another important diplomatic mission as an advisor to Henry VIII. The Field of Cloth and Gold (as it became known) was an eighteen-day festival held near Calais whose high point was a summit meeting between King Henry VIII of England and King Francis I of France (1494–1547). Both were young, well-educated, and athletic men endowed with robust constitutions.[26] King Louis XII of France (1462–1515) had no male heir when he died on January 1, 1515, and he was succeeded by Francis I (r. 1515–1547), son of Charles of Orléans, Count of Angoulême, and Louis XII's son-in-law through Francis' marriage to the king's oldest daughter, Claude (1499–1524). In 1513, Henry VIII invaded France and with the help of the Holy Roman Emperor, Maximilian I, defeated French forces at the Battle of the Spurs.

---

[26] They also died the same year, 1547, within two months of each other.

The English captured the towns of Tornai and Thérouanne—a modest territorial gain for a king who revered warrior-kings like Henry V and Richard the Lionheart and wished to replicate their deeds—but Henry VIII also gained prestige as a military commander. Francis had fought in the armies of Louis XII and solidified his military reputation as king by defeating the Swiss at the Battle of Marignano in September 1515.

Henry VIII was not invited to sign the peace treaty that followed the French victory at Marignano, however, which left the English king sidelined and humiliated. Cardinal Thomas Wolsey (1473—1530), who had arranged a separate peace treaty with France in 1514, mitigated the slight and restored a significant portion of Henry's lost prestige by orchestrating the Treaty of Universal Peace (or Treaty of London), signed in October 1518 by all of the major European powers. This treaty stipulated that Henry VIII and Francis I would meet to ease their personal rivalry, but Emperor Maximilian I died in 1519, and both kings submitted their claims to the imperial throne. It was almost impossible, however, that the electors would choose a candidate outside of the Habsburg family, and the choice fell to the nineteen-year-old King of Spain, Charles V (1500–1558), grandson of Maximilian I and son of a Habsburg archduke. The rivalry between Francis I and Charles V would soon grow to exceed in intensity the rivalry between Francis I and Henry VIII— much of it centered on control of northern Italy. The dispute was only partially settled when, in 1525, an imperial army defeated the French at the Battle of Pavia and captured Francis I. The French king was imprisoned in Spain and forced to make major concessions in the Treaty of Madrid. Once freed, however, Francis formed an alliance with England and repudiated the terms of the treaty despite having previously handed over his two sons as hostages.

Once the imperial election was decided in 1519 and Henry VIII and Francis I were no longer contenders, Wolsey completed the arrangements for the summit meeting at the Field of Cloth and Gold held in 1520. The site was prepared to receive the royal retinues by legions of French and English carpenters, tentmakers, bricklayers, and artisans and artists of all types who constructed elaborate but temporary palaces, courtyards, and pavilions. The structures were erected by placing timber frames upon a foundation of brick and then covering the edifice with stretched canvas, which was then painted to look like stonework or covered with silk woven with gold thread. The temporary buildings also incorporated stained glass, clear glass, terracotta, and ornamental decorations. No expense was spared by either camp to impress the other. The eighteen days were spent in grand celebrations, elaborate feasts, and spectacular tournaments, and it is estimated that twelve thousand people were in attendance. That Thomas More was selected to be a member of the English delegation as a royal counselor cemented his stature as one of the leading men in England.

In 1521, More was knighted and appointed Undertreasurer of the Exchequer, a position greater than any of his previous posts.

According to Erasmus, More did not seek the job but was chosen by the king in preference to another candidate who offered to pay for it. That same year, Henry VIII summoned Edward Stafford, Duke of Buckingham, to London from his Gloucestershire estates. Unbeknownst to Buckingham, the king intended to execute him, and within a month, England's greatest nobleman was beheaded. Stafford, a direct descendant of Edward III, was arrogant in his defense of the ancient feudal rights of the nobility and highly critical of Henry and Wolsey's policies. He disparaged too often and too loudly to remain unnoticed, and among his other indiscretions, he entertained the notion that he might someday become king—a most unwise consideration in light of the queen's inability to bear a male heir and Stafford's relatively young age of forty-four. The trial was conducted in private before a court of the king's ministers. Parliament was not consulted. In earlier times, judicial proceedings of this kind would have been met with outrage and possibly rebellion from the aristocracy given Stafford's high status in English society, but so permanent were the effects of the Wars of the Roses and so thoroughly had Henry VII and Henry VIII tamed the nobility that the trial and summary execution only demonstrated how centralized royal power had become in early-sixteenth-century England. The feat was in fact too easily accomplished, and judicial murders would become a convenient solution to the king's dilemmas for the remainder of his reign.

In 1522, More became Henry's private secretary. Still aspiring to chivalrous glory and military conquest, the king was again considering plans to invade France. More, in keeping with the desire among humanists for peace, advised against it, but Henry and Wolsey had been conspiring with Charles V against Francis I since 1521, and war was resumed in 1522. The emperor sought to force French armies out of northern Italy, while Henry desired to emulate the feats of Henry V and gain for himself territories in France. Wolsey's policy during his years in Henry's service was invariably to fulfill Henry's will, and English armies were once again deployed to France in 1522 and 1523. As in times past, English troops ravaged large areas of the French countryside, but no real advantage was gained and the treasury was exhausted.

Wolsey was forced to summon Parliament in 1523 to secure a grant of taxation. Knowing that a new war subsidy was highly unpopular and would provoke determined resistance, he asked that Thomas More be appointed Speaker of the House so that the request might gain a more favorable hearing. More was reluctant about the war and its cost but acquiesced as a matter of duty. In his first address, he proposed and won greater freedom of speech for members of Parliament, but the war subsidy was a more difficult matter. More and Wolsey eventually prevailed and the grant was passed, but the populace was in no mood to finance Henry's ambitious and largely unsuccessful continental adventures, and his royal commissioners, once having set out to accomplish their unhappy task, met with opposition in the shires and boroughs.

There were other reasons for the inevitable failure of the king's war policy, none of which were lost on his lord chancellor. Wolsey realized that the overriding self-interest of both Henry VIII and Charles V excluded any real possibility that they would coordinate their war efforts, and neither monarch trusted the other. Henry had grown unpopular among his two million subjects, and Wolsey—a wealthy, powerful prelate and the personification of all that needed to be reformed in the Church— had made enemies in his rise to preeminence. Wolsey needed victory in France or peace, and he needed it quickly. A protracted war would mean ruin for Henry's foreign policy and reputation, and the king would remain loyal only if it brought him personal advantage. Wolsey knew he could easily be sacrificed as a scapegoat of failed policy in the way Henry sacrificed his father's unpopular ministers, Edmund Dudley and Richard Empson, by having them executed for treason in 1510. Henry VIII always viewed judicial murder as a royal prerogative.

Toward the end of 1523, Charles Brandon, Duke of Suffolk, was in command of the English armies in France and was ordered to march on Paris, but the campaign failed and ended in the spring of 1524. Then on February 24, 1525 (the emperor's twenty-fifth birthday), the tide of war turned against France when the armies of Charles V defeated French troops who were besieging Pavia and captured Francis I. Charles V could now negotiate with the French king on his own terms. Henry VIII, upon hearing of the victory, was overcome with joy, believing that the crown of France was within his reach—or at the very least, that he might regain the provinces lost during the Hundred Years' War. He quickly sent an English delegation to Spain to negotiate a joint invasion of France, but the mission was unsuccessful. Charles no longer needed Henry and would not agree to the ruin of France, and in any case, neither monarch could afford another costly campaign. Even worse for Henry, Charles revoked his promise to marry Henry's daughter, Princess Mary, which had been given at the signing of the Treaty of Universal Peace, in favor of an offer to marry a Portuguese princess. Henry was once again humiliated, and it was left to Wolsey to devise a plan to assuage the king's bruised ego and repair his damaged reputation at home and abroad. A peace treaty with France was quickly arranged and Henry was left to brood over the duplicity of his imperial nephew. But another problem worried the king even more than this— his lack of a male heir and the problem of royal succession to the English throne, which was becoming more critical each passing year.

~

In 1524, Sir Thomas More was appointed High Steward of Oxford University, and that same year he relocated his family from London to an estate he had built in Chelsea called the "Great House." In 1525, he was appointed High Steward of Cambridge University and Chancellor of the Duchy of Lancaster—one of the king's largest and most important land holdings—and in 1526 he was selected to serve as one of four members of the Royal Council's subcommittee. More's rise in Henry's service coincided with the king's growing concern about the inability of the royal couple to produce a male heir. In 1527, Henry consulted More about the possibility of obtaining an annulment, and later that year, the king finally decided to end his marriage to Catherine. This decision must have been occasioned more readily by Henry's growing attraction to a young courtier, Anne Boleyn (1501–1536), the sister of his former mistress, Mary Boleyn (1499–1543).

While Henry was discussing with his ministers the possibility of obtaining an annulment, momentous news arrived from Italy—imperial troops, hungry and unpaid, had sacked Rome on May 6, 1527, and confined Pope Clement VII at Castel Sant'Angelo. Christendom was again scandalized, and Wolsey and More were sent to France to consolidate the Anglo-French alliance. Henry's desire for an annulment could be settled, Wolsey thought, if he could obtain a papal commission conferring temporary power to act as the pope's vicar in England while Clement VII remained imprisoned, but the plan failed when the pope refused to allow the cardinals, who intended to circumvent his authority, to meet at Avignon. Unbeknownst to Wolsey, the Boleyn and Howard families were conspiring together on a plan of their own to have Anne replace Catherine as queen.

While Wolsey was negotiating in France and unable to influence the king directly, Henry VIII danced and dined with Anne and other members of his court, and his resolve to wed the maiden strengthened. He had been searching Scripture for justification to obtain a dispensation from his marriage vows and found a passage in Leviticus that forbids a man to marry his brother's wife. Since Catherine had once been married to Henry's brother, Arthur, Henry advised Catherine of the possible invalidity of their marriage and insisted that they live apart. Catherine promptly sent a message to her nephew, Charles V, who then pressured Clement VII to declare the marriage valid. This severely limited Wolsey's options. He was the highest-ranking prelate in England,[27] and Henry needed Wolsey's help if he were to have any hope of obtaining an annulment. Wolsey had made a career of obtaining for the king all that he desired—a genius to which Henry had become accustomed—but the cardinal was widely despised for his haughtiness and ostentatious display of wealth and power. He had made enemies among the nobility who were jealous of his power and believed it should be theirs. And he also faced intrigue and opposition at court from his enemies in the Boleyn faction who were jealous of his influence over the king. To complicate matters further, Catherine was popular among the English, and she was protesting the divorce vehemently. In the end, the task was too formidable and Wolsey would fail in the "king's great matter," a shortcoming for which he would not be forgiven.

But the great man of affairs of Church and state had not yet shot his final bolt. Wolsey returned to England at the conclusion of the negotiations in France and busied himself with the divorce.

---

[27] Wolsey was the Primate of England in virtue of his office as the Cardinal Archbishop of York.

His plans were disrupted, however, when news arrived from the continent of the imperial victory over the French at the Battle of Landriano on June 21, 1529, which sealed Charles V's victory at Pavia and his control of northern Italy. The dispute between Francis I and Charles V had been settled, and an end to the quarrel between Charles V and Clement VII was soon to follow in the Treaty of Barcelona signed on June 29, 1529. While these discussions were taking place, Louise of Savoy (Francis I's mother) and Margaret of Austria (Charles V's aunt) met at Cambrai to finalize a peace agreement (later called the Ladies' Peace) between the empire and France. Neither Francis I nor Charles V wanted to include England in the deliberations, and Wolsey, who had recently been appointed by the pope to a commission as papal legate along with Cardinal Lorenzo Campeggio to examine the royal marriage, was caught unawares by the discussions at Cambrai. Once informed, and being unable to travel because of the divorce proceedings in London, he hurriedly sent Thomas More and Bishop Cuthbert Tunstall to Cambrai on June 30. By the time they arrived over a week later, however, the substance of the negotiations was already concluded. The English delegation was left to salvage from the mission what they could and were modestly successful in preserving trade provisions between England and the Low Countries that were previously in place.

If the Peace of Cambrai signed in August 1529 marked the ruin of Henry VIII and Cardinal Wolsey's foreign policy, for humanists like Thomas More, it was a victory for peace. More considered Cambrai the most important diplomatic mission of his career, and it gave him so much personal satisfaction that he included a reference to it in the epitaph he wrote before his death which he intended to be displayed at his grave in Chelsea.

Wolsey's dilemma, on the other hand, grew more dire. Before More and Tunstall returned home from Cambrai, the final meeting of the court presided over by Cardinal Campeggio that was to determine the validity of the royal marriage was adjourned by Campeggio without a verdict, and the decision was secretly recalled to Rome. It is clear in hindsight that the pope never intended to reverse the original dispensation that allowed Henry and Catherine to marry. The king's hopes in this matter, like his foreign policy, were doomed to failure, and Wolsey's position now was hopeless. His star, so long in the ascendant, was now in rapid decline and his fifteen years at the summit of affairs of Church and state were coming to an end.

15

Mission Sequence
Lord Chancellor (1529 to 1532)

In October 1529, Cardinal Wolsey was indicted on a charge of *praemunire* (allegiance to a foreign power, specifically the pope) and relieved of his state duties and ecclesiastical offices, except as Archbishop of York. Henry VIII consulted with members of his council to discuss Wolsey's replacement, and it was decided that the next lord chancellor should be a layman rather than a cleric to avoid the creation of another Wolsey. A layman would not have the ecclesiastical revenues that would enable him to rival the king in splendor as Wolsey had done, nor would he be as offensive to the nobility who believed that only great lords should exercise the power Wolsey possessed (Wolsey was a commoner and the son of an Ipswich butcher). The choice of a layman would also send an unmistakable message to Rome at a time when the issue of the annulment was still officially undecided. Thomas More emerged as the candidate of choice even though he dissented from the king's opinion on the validity of the royal marriage. Perhaps Henry thought he could eventually overcome More's resistance

111

and oblige him to obedience by the force of his personality and conviction; or perhaps he hoped that More would someday defer to the theological opinion of the churchmen who supported Henry's position; or he may have presumed that More would eventually acquiesce out of a sense of duty and loyalty to the king. In any case, More received the Great Seal of England on October 25, 1529, and assumed the duties of England's highest-ranking minister.

Historians and biographers have speculated over More's reasons for accepting the lord chancellorship when he knew that Henry, who wished to rule as *rex et imperator*, was determined to have his way in the matter of the annulment. More had said on a previous occasion that his head would not fail to roll if the king would receive a castle in France for it. Did he not think it would roll if his death would further Henry's plans for obtaining an annulment? More was also aware that Parliament was being called into session and that Henry was prepared to bully and intimidate them into passing legislation he intended to propose. Did More not realize that he might one day be subject to the same treatment?

More knew Henry as well as any person in England—except for, perhaps, Queen Catherine—and he must have realized that acceptance of the lord chancellorship might someday cost him his life. Yet he had already shown during his professional career and as a royal servant that he was motivated by reasons higher than mere self-interest or self-preservation. And he had earned a reputation among his peers and in the city of London as a man of integrity who sought service to the realm and promotion of the common good rather than wealth or power for himself. His motivations were summed up in a letter he wrote to Erasmus in October 1529 in which he confided that he accepted the appointment "in the interest of Christendom." Genuine altruism was, therefore, a motivating factor in More's decision, but it must have been accompanied by an awareness that the lord chancellorship was the culmination of a path he had walked since birth (*life journey*), and that his formation and life experiences converged on this decision. He was surely motivated by a sense of duty and probably felt morally obliged to assent to the king's request as the next phase of a divinely ordained plan which included a personal mission that only he could fulfill.

More did not serve the king for his own aggrandizement as did many of his peers, but he accepted what came to him as ordained by Providence, and discerned God's will in the manner he discerned his vocation to marriage and family. We may therefore identify three motivating factors that led More to accept the lord chancellorship:

1. Commitment to service to the Kingdom of England and the Church (altruism)

2. Culmination of a path in life he had walked since birth (predestiny)

3. Obedience to God's will and the fulfillment of his personal mission (duty).

~

Historians have noted a significant difference between the Protestant Reformation begun by Luther in 1517 and the English Reformation initiated by Henry VIII in the 1530s. The Protestant Reformation has been described primarily as a *religious reformation* (originating with a doctrinal dispute over the Church's theology on indulgences) which had *political ramifications* (e.g. German Peasants' Revolt in 1524). Conversely, the English Reformation has been described primarily as a *political reformation* (beginning in 1531 with the creation of Henry's title as the Supreme Head of the Church of England, later confirmed by Parliament in the Act of Supremacy of 1534) which had *religious ramifications* (i.e., the formation of the Anglican Church).

The Parliament that assembled at Blackfriars Church on November 3, 1529, just days after More's appointment as lord chancellor, is known to history as the Reformation Parliament (1529–1536) and serves as a suitable starting point for the political revolution that followed. It was customary for the lord chancellor to give an opening speech before the combined Houses of Lords and Commons, and Sir Thomas More, with the king in attendance, announced that Parliament had been called into session to "reform abuses" of ecclesiastical privileges. More was also virtually obliged as Henry's highest-ranking minister to denounce his predecessor, which he did in vague terms, censuring Wolsey for being crafty and fraudulent in his relations with the king but making no specific mention of any of the abuses which were so liberally attributed to him by his enemies. Once the largely rhetorical denunciation had been issued, More's final task in the opening address was to request that Parliament elect a speaker, and Thomas Audley—who had replaced More as Chancellor of the Duchy of Lancaster and would someday replace him as Lord Chancellor of England—was chosen.

A debate then arose in the House of Commons in which the usual grievances against the clergy were again aired. The result was the passage of legislation that required all clergy members[28] to be tried in common law courts rather than in canonical courts where they were treated with greater leniency. This measure was the first of a series of laws that Henry used to pressure Clement VII into declaring the king's marriage null. The campaign against clerical abuses continued in a bill called the Supplication of the Commons in which the clergy were reprimanded by the House of Commons for their "insatiable" greed. The bishops responded in the customary manner by comparing the dissenters to Lutherans and Hussites and arguing that if obedience were withdrawn from Church authority, it would soon be withheld from civil authority. Bishop John Fisher of Rochester spoke in defense of the Church's rights and was later summoned by the king to defend his comments.

---

[28] The clergy at this time consisted of any member of the four minor orders (porter, lector, exorcist, and acolyte) and the three major or "sacred" orders (subdeacon, deacon, and priest).

A Hero Is Chosen

16

Turning Point
Capitulation of the Clergy and Resignation
Thomas' Hero-Event

The political revolution that was unfolding in England beginning in 1529 alarmed More, whose concern had always been to combat heresy and preserve the traditional Church. He perceived in Henry's assault on the clergy a threat to the ancient order of Christendom that went far beyond what humanists of his kind were advocating. More rejected Luther and the other reformers in part because they promoted division rather than unity and fostered a breakdown of traditional authority that had long been a guarantee of European civilization. Christian humanists like More sought the reform of abuses and the correction of errors through "sound learning," but they stopped short of advocating rebellion. Reform had limits for men like More, and he was not willing to dispense with centuries-old tradition.

~

After Cardinal Wolsey had been relieved of his offices and benefices (except for the archbishopric of York), he moved his residence to Yorkshire in April 1530 to govern the archdiocese as its bishop. It was the first time in his long career that he had been to York, but he would not remain there long. Despite his many enemies who would have done away with him much sooner, he continued to enjoy the king's protection, but it was only a matter of time, and on November 4, Wolsey was charged with treason and ordered to report to the Tower of London. He would not complete the journey, however, and probably to the king's satisfaction, he died in Leicester on November 29—saved no doubt from the block. He is reported to have said before his passing, "If I had served God as diligently as I have the king, he would not have given me over in my grey hairs." Perhaps God had other plans than to hand him over "in his grey hairs." Wolsey had in fact been living a more faithful spiritual life in the months preceding his death, probably with the recognition that his enemies would eventually have their way. In any case, his downfall and death were yet another sign that the winds of change were blowing in England and that one era was passing away and another about to begin.

Another sign of the changing times was the death of Sir John More, who passed within days of Cardinal Wolsey. After his father's death, Thomas More confessed to feeling old and began to suffer from pain in his chest (probably angina). His weariness would last another five years until he followed them into eternity, but unlike Wolsey, he would not escape the block.

~

The wave of anticlericalism that arose after Wolsey's fall in October 1529 gained momentum in the Parliament that convened in November 1529 and renewed itself when Parliament was again called into session in January 1531. Henry had taken Thomas Cromwell into his service during the recess, and Cromwell would henceforth become the architect of the king's policy. Under his guidance, the king was now prepared to take a more determined role in directing the passage of legislation. Henry first insisted that the clergy atone for their greed and fiscal abuses by paying the expenses that the king incurred in attempting to procure an annulment from Rome. He then charged them with *praemunire* for having tried cases in ecclesiastical courts rather than common law courts and demanded that the Convocation of the Clergy acknowledge him as "sole protector and supreme head of the English Church and clergy." The bishops balked at the caesaropapist title, and Bishop Fisher asked what would happen if "a woman came to the throne." But the king prevailed in February 1531 when the Convocation consented to a decree that acknowledged Henry (with one important caveat that made it less distressing but no less precarious) as "their singular protector, only and supreme Lord, and so far as the law of Christ allows, even Supreme Head."

Parliament was prorogued for a time but reconvened in April 1532. A bill was passed restricting the payment of annates to Rome and the Commons issued the Supplication against the

Ordinaries (Bishops) asking the king to remedy a list of clerical offenses. Henry promised to be impartial, and when the bishops replied that ecclesiastical courts were under God's authority and not the king's, Henry responded by declaring to the Commons, "We think their answer will smally please you, for it seemeth to us very slender." And he asserted:

> [W]e thought that the clergy of our realm had been our subjects wholly; but now we all well perceive that they be but half our subjects—yea, and scarce our subjects. For all the prelates at their consecration make an oath to the Pope clean contrary to the oath they make to us, so that they seem his subjects and not ours.

Henry had thus far been unable to prevail over Clement in the matter of the annulment, distant as the pope was in his palace in Rome and largely unaffected by Henry's royal authority, but the English king's power was more effectually exercised over the clergy in his realm, and under Cromwell's guidance, he pressed his advantage. The campaign to break the resistance of the clergy and destroy what remained of their independence advanced to another assault on canon law. If the king could become master of ecclesiastical law in England, he would become master of the Church in England. In May 1532, Henry demanded that Parliament grant him the right to form a committee composed of lay and clerical members tasked with examining individual canons and endowed with the authority to discard those that were not in accord with English common law or the king's prerogatives. Henry further required that any revision to canon law could only become effective by royal consent. This legislation aimed to: (a) attain for the king full sovereignty over Church affairs, (b) give precedence to English common law over canon law, and (c) make common law courts superior to ecclesiastical courts—all of which amounted to a repudiation of papal jurisdiction. But Henry could not accomplish this lawfully without the voluntary consent of Parliament and the Convocation of the Clergy. As the Convocation was considering the king's demands, Henry increased the pressure by sending his councilors to bully and intimidate them with the threat of even more drastic measures. The gambit succeeded, and on May 15, the clergy capitulated. Henry's victory was decisive.

The clergy's submission in 1532 would have far-reaching and enduring consequences, one of which was to make Thomas More's position untenable. It was clear that Henry intended to use his authority to have his marriage to Catherine declared invalid and thereby procure his own annulment. More could no longer walk the middle path of obedience to the pope and service to the king, and his conscience would not allow him to change his position on the validity of the royal marriage. On Thursday, May 16, 1532, and with no viable alternative, Thomas More traveled to the royal residence at York Place—a palace that once belonged to Cardinal Wolsey but was confiscated by the king after Wolsey's fall from power—and was escorted to the garden where Henry was waiting with Thomas Howard, Duke of Norfolk and Lord Treasurer. More exchanged the requisite pleasantries with the two men before handing over to Henry a pouch containing the Great Seal of England, and in so doing, resigned as lord chancellor.

~

Thomas More served Henry VIII for twelve years before he became lord chancellor, an office he occupied for three years. He then spent three years in retirement until his martyrdom in 1535. For those who are interested in Biblical numerology, twelve and three are highly significant numbers. Also noteworthy was that he resigned at three o'clock in the afternoon, the hour at which Christ died on the cross.

There are no coincidences for those who pray.

~

In late May 1532, Henry sent a group of royal councilors to Queen Catherine at Greenwich Palace to dissuade her from appealing to the pope, but she refused. Henry renounced the marriage on July 11, and on September 1, he ennobled Anne Boleyn as the Marchioness of Pembroke. Later that autumn, she informed him that she was pregnant.

On January 26, 1533, Thomas Audley, who had been Keeper of the Great Seal of England since Thomas More's resignation, was appointed lord chancellor. Parliament assembled again in January 1533, the same month that Henry and Anne were privately married at York Place. Thomas Cromwell worked diligently with Parliament to pass the Act of Restraint of Appeals to Rome, which it finally did on April 7, 1533, after much debate. This bill was initially meant to prevent the pope from interfering in the royal divorce, but the final draft was broadened to disavow papal authority within the king's realm by decreeing that all of the king's subjects were exclusively under royal jurisdiction.

Henry and Cromwell wasted no time after gaining this legislative victory and arranged for a trial to determine the validity of the royal marriage, the first session of which was to be held on May 10 at Dunstable Priory. The outcome was never in doubt, as Henry's councilors served as the judges. Thomas Cranmer, the newly appointed Archbishop of Canterbury, presided over the proceedings and summoned Henry and Catherine to appear before the court, but the queen refused to attend. The "king's great matter" was finally put to rest on May 23 (at least as far as Henry was concerned) when Cranmer officially declared the marriage contrary to the law of God and therefore null, and within a week he confirmed the validity of Henry's marriage to Anne Boleyn. Henry had previously ordered that grand celebrations begin the day following the announcement so that London might welcome its new queen, and four days of festivities began when Anne sailed the Thames from Greenwich to the Tower of London. She was crowned Queen of England at Westminster Abbey on June 1, 1533.

Thomas More was invited to the coronation by a few of his bishop-friends, including his former diplomatic colleague, Bishop

Cuthbert Tunstall (who had published a book on mathematics in 1522 which he dedicated to More), but he declined the invitation. More's absence did not go unnoticed, and Henry may have taken it as an act of defiance. When More resigned the lord chancellorship in May 1532, he left in the king's good graces, but his friendship with Henry was (as all the king's friendships were) contingent on supplying the king with what he wanted. Wolsey was the first in a line of royal ministers who were discarded by Henry despite having served him faithfully—in Wolsey's case, he was unable to procure a declaration of nullity from Rome—and it was only his unexpected death on the journey to London that prevented him from a trip to the scaffold. More followed Wolsey in provoking the king's displeasure by his unwillingness to assent to the nullity of his marriage to Catherine and his refusal to acknowledge Henry's legal or moral right to declare it himself. This resistance eventually became intolerable to Henry, which he viewed as tantamount to treason. Anne's coronation marks a turning point when Henry's attitude toward More became increasingly hostile.

On July 11, 1533, Pope Clement VII condemned the royal divorce, threatened Henry with excommunication, and ordered him to reunite with Catherine. Henry replied by appealing to a general council. On September 7, Anne gave birth to a child he hoped would be a male heir, and the offspring she bore him would indeed someday rule England, but she would not be his son. Elizabeth I, the last of the Tudor monarchs, succeeded her half-brother, Edward VI (r. 1547–1553) and her half-sister, Mary I

(r. 1553–1558), and reigned as Queen of England from 1558 until 1603. In one of the great ironies of history, Henry VIII, once awarded the title "Defender of the Faith by the pope, was willing to sever England from Rome and suffer the penalty of excommunication (and thereby risk his salvation) in order to gain a male heir so that his kingdom might not descend into civil war or become a dominion of a foreign ruler through marriage. Elizabeth, for her part, never married a foreign prince, safeguarded England from foreign invasion, and is credited by historians as having reigned during one of the most stable and glorious periods in English history.

~

And there is a lesson in this with respect to service to God, discipleship of Christ, and hero-sainthood: It is sometimes better to "let God be God" and allow him to take care of the "impossible" details and future contingencies than to attempt too strenuously to direct the course of human events. And it is sometimes better to trust in Providence and wait for a Deus ex machina moment than to rely too heavily on our plans or those of our neighbor. And it is never permissible in the moral life to perform an evil action in order to procure a desired good, no matter how valuable that good may appear. And it is never wise to press too hard to open a door that cannot be opened except through sin and rebellion. Obedience is the better part of valor, and it is best to let God write those parts of our life story (or hero story) that are beyond our ability to control. Henry VIII might have become a great saint, and even a hero-saint, but he instead became a tyrant.

~

By February 1534, Henry could no longer tolerate More's silent intransigence, and probably at the urging of Anne, who felt snubbed at More's absence from her coronation, he asked the House of Lords for an indictment. The king insisted that More and Fisher's names be included on a Bill of Attainder against Elizabeth Barton, the "Holy Maid of Kent," who had prophesied against Henry regarding his divorce of Catherine. Barton was charged with treason and later executed, and both More and Fisher had previously associated with the nun. Parliament, however, refused three times to pass the bill and More's name was withdrawn. But the king was nonetheless determined…

In March 1534, Parliament passed the Act of Succession, which required all English subjects to accept Henry's marriage to Anne as valid and recognize their offspring as Henry's lawful successors. This meant the repudiation of the rights of Catherine's daughter, Mary Tudor (who, despite Henry's best efforts, would someday reign as Queen Mary I). The king demoted Catherine to the title of Dowager Princess of Wales and banished her from his court, consigning her first to Buckden and later to Kimbolton as a form of internal exile. She remained popular among the English, however, and many of Henry's subjects still considered her to be the queen. The revolution that Henry and his ministers were forcing on England was not universally accepted—especially among religious orders and those who remained faithful to the pope—and many of the bills that were passed through Parliament did so only by narrow margins.

17

Desert Experience
Imprisonment

Once Parliament passed the Act of Succession, Henry's ministers began summoning high-ranking clergymen to appear at Lambeth Palace to take the Oath of Succession. On April 12, 1534, Thomas More was at Saint Paul's Cathedral in London with his son-in-law, William Roper, when he received an official summons to appear at Lambeth the following morning. He returned to Chelsea to bid his family farewell and inform them that he would likely be imprisoned. The next morning, he attended Mass at his parish church where he received communion and confessed to a priest, after which he boarded a small boat and, accompanied by Roper, was transported by water to Lambeth. As they were being rowed down the Thames, More whispered to Roper, "I thank the Lord that the field is won."

When it was More's turn to appear before the royal commissioners at Lambeth, he asked to read the Oath and the Act of Succession. Having examined both carefully, he stated that he would swear allegiance to Henry and Anne as the King and Queen of England and recognize their offspring as successors to the throne, since Parliament, he believed, had the power to enact this into law, but he refused to swear the Oath as it was written claiming that it was against his conscience to do so. More would not specify beyond this, but it is thought that he objected to a statement in the preamble of the Act which asserted that Henry and Catherine's marriage was invalid, as well as to elements of the Oath which required the renunciation of papal authority. The commissioners committed More to the custody of the Abbot of Westminster while they consulted with Henry. The king, however, would not accept a compromise, and on April 17, More was imprisoned in the Tower of London.

Parliament met again in November 1534 and passed the Act Respecting the Oath to the Succession which required all of Henry's subjects to take an oath to uphold the Act of Succession. Parliament also passed the Act of Supremacy which enshrined into law Henry's title of Supreme Head of the Church of England without the provision "so far as the law of Christ allows." The break with Rome was now complete and Henry had displaced the pope as the Vicar of Christ within his realm. To make noncompliance punishable by death, Henry and Cranmer cajoled Parliament to pass the Treason Act which made it seditious to refuse to take the Oath of Succession or disavow the Act of Supremacy.

"This world of reformation"—a phrase coined by Thomas Cranmer—was moving inexorably away from the world which

Thomas More was trying to preserve. He remained imprisoned in the Tower with Bishop John Fisher who also refused compliance, awaiting in separate cells the destiny they would share. More's accommodations at first were not severe and he was allowed a servant, writing materials, and visits from his daughter, Margaret, and eventually his wife, Alice. He wrote numerous works while in prison including *A Dialogue of Comfort against Tribulation* and *A Treatise on the Passion* (which he did not complete) as well as touching letters to Margaret. Henry and his advisors allowed these privileges hoping that More would succumb to the entreaties of family and friends and utter those few words that meant the difference between life and death, but that day never came. Despite the lengthy exchanges between More and his family members, he was unable to convince them of the rightness of his convictions, nor were they able to understand his willingness to sacrifice his life when most of England's prelates had already conceded to the king. When questioned by Cromwell regarding his position on the Act of Supremacy, More refrained from commenting and claimed that he did not wish to meddle in other people's consciences, as this might force them into a moral dilemma and imperil their salvation.

On May 4, 1535, the Carthusians John Houghton, Prior of the Charterhouse in London; Robert Lawrence, Prior of Beauvale; and Augustine Webster, Prior of Axholme; along with the Bridgettine, Richard Reynolds of Syon Abbey, and John Haile, a secular priest, were led from their prison cells in the Tower of London, tied to hurdles, and dragged to Tyburn to be hanged, drawn, and quartered for their refusal to assent to the Act of Supremacy. More watched from the window of his cell and listened until the men were taken out of sight. Margaret was with him, weeping and begging him to reconsider, but contrary to the hope of his captors, the experience only strengthened More's resolve.

Clement VII passed away on September 25, 1534, and was succeeded as pope by Paul III (r. 1534–1549). Henry and his councilors wondered if the change in papal leadership might induce conciliation from Rome but were confounded when Paul III elevated Fisher to the cardinalate on May 20, 1535. An enraged Henry vowed to behead him "before the hat arrived," which meant that imprisonment was not a long-term option for either Fisher or More. Both men had become international symbols of resistance to the king's will, and Henry would not tolerate insubordination. The sands of time were slipping through the hourglass as the course of human events unfolded…

Cromwell continued to meet with More inquiring about his opinion of the Act and Oath of Supremacy, but More would not change his position or give a direct answer. There seemed to be no solution to the stalemate. More had in fact been imprisoned illegally since there was no evidence to convict him of a crime, yet his and Fisher's civil disobedience (or Christian noncompliance) was providing a public example of dissent from royal policy. The impasse was finally resolved (so to speak) when the Solicitor General, Richard Rich, was sent by Cromwell on June 12, 1535, to confiscate More's books and papers after it was discovered that More and Fisher were communicating. The two lawyers began an informal conversation about the law as it pertained to his case, which More assumed was an abstract discussion regarding hypotheticals. But Rich intended to lay a trap and reported to Cromwell a statement that More allegedly made regarding Parliament's lack of power to pass the Act of Supremacy. More later denied having questioned the king's title as Supreme Head, but the royal councilors were determined to use this allegation against him before a jury.

Fisher was being interrogated in the Tower on the same day that Rich visited More. Both men were employing a strategy of silence, but Fisher had on an earlier occasion been asked to give his honest opinion about the king's supremacy and was promised by Henry that no harm would come to him if he answered truthfully. This was also a trap, and after having answered candidly, Fisher was tried and found guilty on June 17 of denying the king's supremacy. He would have suffered the same fate at Tyburn as the Carthusians, but in poor health and approaching death, his sentence was commuted by the king to beheading.

Cardinal John Fisher thus gave his life to God on June 22, 1535, and as was the custom, his head was impaled on a pole and displayed on London Bridge. The cardinal's hat, however, was not to rest upon it until he reached Paradise.

18

Capstone Experience
Trial and Tower Hill
Thomas More's Hero-Moment

More wrote one of his last letters in June 1535, just days before his trial which began on July 1. It was to Antonio Bonvisi, an Italian merchant and fellow humanist who he had known for almost forty years and one of his closest friends. Despite the danger to his own person and property, Bonvisi had been sending provisions to More and Fisher while they were imprisoned in the Tower. The letter was written in Latin, and since More had no pen or ink at this time, he wrote it using a piece of coal—just as he did with his last letter to Margaret (Meg) on July 5, the day before his execution.

~

The trial of Sir Thomas More is one of the most celebrated in English history. Fifteen judges and twelve jurors assembled on July 1, 1535, at Westminster Hall to convict a man (for there was never any doubt as to the verdict) who, like Socrates over a thousand years earlier, preferred to sacrifice his life than surrender his integrity.

Fisher's life journey was now over, and More stood alone. A Londoner among Londoners, a friend among strangers he had known for years, an Englishman among Englishmen of a dissimilar breed, reform-minded men of an altogether different brand. Alone he stood, against a king he once served who now sought his life, prosecuted within a legal system he had with incorruptibility upheld, and even now revered. The law he had safeguarded was being twisted against him to placate the will of a tyrant, a man he once befriended—even if More was never naive about the limits and quality of that friendship.

The bishops still alive had all abandoned his cause, having capitulated to preserve life and liberty, income and status. His family, having enjoyed for years his pious company and learned conversation, could now not comprehend his resolve when most of his peers and theologians of a higher grade than himself had bowed to the king's demands. Even the daughterly affections of dear Meg were used by his captors against him, to soften him, that he might yield to familial sympathies and the weakness of the flesh. But he would not surrender his sanctity.

His hair was longer now, and a beard covered his once fresh and lively face. Eyes grown soft and tired, leaner of body, a weary and much older man than the one who arrived at Lambeth Palace fifteen months ago. Lambeth Palace. Where he had served as a page in the household of Archbishop Morton. Where he learned the etiquette and manners of high society. Where he met other boys and young men who would grow up to be like the men who were now opposing him.

Alone he stood, surrounded by accusers and judges. A man already convicted for remaining faithful to his convictions, a man of principle dedicated to principles—legal, moral, and religious. A man who would not compromise his beliefs in the unity and universality of the Church and the inviolability of its spiritual authority, and the rights and limits of kings and parliaments on laws they may justly pass to inhibit it. And above all else, a man who would not compromise his conscience.

The trial began and the indictment was read. Lord Chancellor Audley then offered More the king's mercy if he would repent of his obstinacy. More replied by appealing to God for the strength to maintain his "honest mind" and reminding the judges of his ill health and weakness. He was given a chair on which to sit.

Joan of Arc, at the behest of her voices, replied boldly at her trial one hundred and four years earlier. Thomas More, a deft legal tactician, answered skillfully at his. The charges against him were arrayed in four articles:

1. More's refusal to accept royal supremacy over the English Church, his denial of Parliament's authority to grant it by law, and his treason in maintaining the pope's authority to govern the Church in England.

2. His correspondence with Fisher, a known traitor, while both were in prison, in which he instructed and encouraged Fisher in his treasonous behavior.

3. His refusal to accept the nullity of the king's marriage to Catherine, which implied a refusal to accept the validity of the king's marriage to Anne Boleyn.

4. His refusal to give a clear and straightforward answer when asked by the king's representatives regarding his opinion on royal supremacy, which was interpreted as a sign of malicious intent against the king.

To these charges, More pleaded "not guilty" and argued that:

1. Parliament had the authority to pass laws regarding the succession to the throne of England, and he was prepared to accept Henry and Anne as lawful king and queen and swear allegiance to their successors.

2. As to the matter of Henry's right to rule the Church of England in place of the pope, More declined to give his opinion because it was a matter of conscience and he had not yet, nor did he ever intend to, disclose his "conscience and mind to any person living in the whole world."

3. It was impossible to prove that he had encouraged Fisher in treasonous activity in their correspondence while in prison because there was no evidence to support it. Fisher had burned the letters, and More could only disclose the contents that he remembered, none of which pointed to treasonous activity.

4. He had never maliciously resisted the king's marriage to Anne Boleyn while in office or after his resignation, and when asked by Henry while he was the king's minister, he had answered honestly and truthfully according to his conscience, and for this he cannot be blamed, for if he had done otherwise, he would have been an unfaithful councilor. As to why he kept silent about certain matters, More responded that this was a matter of conscience and:

  a. The disclosure of his conscience might inform the conscience of others who might thereby incur guilt by being placed in a moral dilemma that would require them to make the same moral choice he was making—a choice that might also require them to make the same sacrifice he was making (which they might not be willing to make, thus incurring guilt).

  b. Matters of conscience are more important "than any other thing in all the world beside" and he had a moral and religious right to refrain from disclosing his conscience.

  c. He was commended by the king when he resigned as lord chancellor to concern himself with the salvation of his soul and to prepare for death, a task with which he was now fully occupied, and which did not require him to be involved in the affairs of state.

5. It is morally justifiable from a religious perspective to keep silent about matters of conscience and those "inward things" that pertain to God. From a legal perspective, silence is usually interpreted as a sign of consent, and if interpreted so in his case, he would be innocent of the

charge of malice, and that "for this my silence neither your law nor any law in the world is able justly and rightly to punish me."

There was nothing new in the charges brought against More or in his defense. The evidence against him had always been flimsy and the case unsound, except that Richard Rich now appeared to testify against him. Rich stated that More denied that Henry was the Supreme Head of the Church of England and that Parliament had no authority to enact legislation that made him so. Two other men had accompanied Rich to More's cell that day—Sir Richard Southwell and John Palmer—but they were busy confiscating More's books and writing materials while More and Rich were conversing, and both men testified that they could not corroborate Rich's testimony. More denied having made the statement and accused Rich of perjury, asserting that he would never have revealed his conscience to a man of Rich's inferior rank, especially pertaining to matters he would not reveal to the king or members of the royal council. Yet, he maintained, even if he had denied the king's supremacy, there would have been no malice involved since he harbored no malice against the king, but only friendship, and "where there is no malice, there can be no offense."

But there was never a doubt as to the verdict, and after deliberating for less than an hour, the jury found More guilty. Before he was sentenced, Audley asked him if he had any final comments. It was a moment for which he was prepared.

Thomas More never sought to die a martyr as have others in Christian history, and he probably did not consider his death a martyrdom. He did what he could to avoid being executed without sacrificing his conscience or convictions, and when he saw that there was no other choice but to accept death at the hands of men he sincerely wished were his friends, he spoke to "discharge of my conscience and speak my mind plainly and freely touching my indictment and your Statute withal." He then stated that the "Act of Parliament" which served as the grounds for his conviction was "directly repugnant to the laws of God and his holy Church" and that:

> [N]o temporal prince [may] presume by any law to take upon himself, as rightfully belonging to the See of Rome, a spiritual pre-eminence by the mouth of our Savior himself, personally present upon earth, only to Saint Peter and his successors, bishops of the same see, by special prerogative granted.

Audley replied that this was contrary to the opinion of the English bishops and theologians who had sided with the king. More responded that they represented only a small portion of the bishops and theologians of the universal Church, most of whom would disagree, and that the vast majority of the "holy saints in heaven" could be counted on to agree with his position, and for this reason, he was not in the minority. Therefore, he asserted:

> I am not bound, my Lord, to conform my conscience to the council of one realm against the general council of Christendom... For I have all the councils made these

thousand years. And for this one kingdom, I have all other Christian realms.

Thomas Howard, Duke of Norfolk, then said, "We plainly see that ye are maliciously bent!" To which More responded:

[T]he discharge of my conscience enforceth me to speak so much. Wherein I call and appeal to God, whose only sight pierceth into the very depth of man's heart, to be my witness. Howbeit, it is not for this Supremacy so much that ye seek my blood, as for that I would not condescend to the marriage.

Audley fell silent for a moment. He turned to Sir John FitzJames, Lord Chief Justice, and asked if the indictment was sufficient. FitzJames responded with a statement containing two double negatives that ended the debate: "My Lords ... if the act of Parliament be not unlawful, then the indictment is not in my conscience invalid." And with this mystifying rejoinder, Thomas More's destiny was sealed and the Great Game on this occasion came to a close. Evil had won another battle ... but not the war.[29]

More was asked again if he had any final comments. He referred to the passage in Acts of the Apostles (8:1) where Paul gave his consent to the stoning of Stephen, and More reminded his judges that both men were now saints and "friends forever" in heaven:

---

[29] As earlier stated, when Thomas More and William Roper were being rowed down the Thames to Lambeth Palace before More was imprisoned, More whispered to Roper: "I thank the Lord that the field is won."

So I verily trust, and shall therefore right heartily pray, that though your Lordships have now here on earth been judges to my condemnation, may we yet hereafter in Heaven merrily all meet together, to our everlasting salvation.

~

He was sentenced to be hanged, drawn, and quartered at Tyburn, as were the Carthusians who preceded him to the gallows. He was not ashamed to be counted among their number in death and would have gladly been counted with them in life and shared their monastic journey, but he had another call to answer. We may fairly wonder if the inscrutable ordinances of Providence were otherwise, and if he were destined to join the ranks of the blessed Carthusians, that a man of More's quality and character might well have risen to the rank of prior, and perhaps on an earlier occasion in that "world of reformation," he might have been dragged by horse and hurdle to the gallows at Tyburn clad in white wool robe and cowl. Yet by some great mystery not yet apprehended by mortals still subject to these earthly confines, he was called to be companioned with them, if not in life, then in death, and to share forever in their illustrious fame.

~

More was escorted back to Tower Wharf from Westminster by the Constable of the Tower, Sir William Kingston—a tall, strong, and handsome knight and a good friend of More's. When the short conveyance was at an end and as they were bidding each other farewell, Kingston began to weep with heaviness of heart. Upon seeing this, More consoled him:

> Good Master Kingston, trouble not yourself, but be of good cheer, for I will pray for you and my good Lady, your wife, that we may meet in heaven together, where we shall be merry for ever and ever.

As More climbed out of the boat onto the wharf, he was met by Margaret and her husband, William Roper. Roper later wrote that Margaret hastened to him, and with no regard for her personal safety or the crowd, pressed "in among the midst of the throng and company of the guard that with halberds and bills went round about him," and "there openly, in the sight of them all, embraced him, took him about the neck, and kissed him." More comforted her: "Have patience, Margaret, and trouble not thyself. It is the will of God. Long hast thou known the secrets of my heart." After a moment of tears and sadness, Margaret withdrew ten paces, but "having respect neither to herself, nor to the press of the people and multitude that were there about him, suddenly turned back again, ran to him as before, took him about the neck, and divers times together most lovingly kissed him."

More asked her to pray for his soul.

~

His last few days were spent in the same cold, dank prison cell. Cromwell came again for one last, vain attempt, but More would not yield his conscience. On July 5, the day before he was to die, his wife Alice was permitted a visit. More entrusted to her his final letter to Margaret, written with a piece of coal. In it, he said, "I never liked your manner toward me better than when you kissed me last; for I love when daughterly love and dear charity hath no leisure to look to worldly courtesy."

~

The terrors of Tyburn would be spared him, but More would receive neither pardon nor reprieve. In a moment of humanity, and befitting his rank, the king commuted More's sentence to beheading on Tower Hill.

~

Milk Street, the place of his birth and childhood, was not far from the site of his execution, and the full circle of his life from birth to death was coming to completion less than a mile apart. The irony of his life would have it so. Thomas was born into law and he was destined to practice it as a livelihood, and it was by the law—or an exploitation of it—that he would die. He had traveled abroad but was never at home, even among fellow humanists, except when in London. A true citizen of London as much as any person could be, it was only fitting that he die there. The king he had faithfully served had faithlessly sought his condemnation, and Thomas Becket, with whom More shared a name and birthplace, would now share with him an even finer distinction.

On July 6, 1535—the eve of the Feast of the Translation of Saint Thomas Becket—and shortly before 9:00 am, More was escorted to the scaffold just two hundred yards from his cell. A crowd had gathered to witness the spectacle, and the noise and commotion that assailed More's senses in these final moments must have contrasted sharply with the silence, solitude, and dreariness of the endless days of imprisonment he had endured over the past fifteen months. As he walked the path to Tower Hill, a conflicting sense of impending doom must have mingled with a hint of relief and the knowledge that his life was ending in so honorable a manner.

Among those who accompanied him to the scaffold was Humphrey Monmouth, one of the Sheriffs of London. More had once interrogated Monmouth over heresy and confined him to the Tower. The irony of Monmouth's presence at More's execution was apparently intended by his oppressors, as was the slight, and the circle of More's life was coming to a close.

~

The king demanded through a messenger, Thomas Pope, a friend of More's, that More's last words be brief. The condemned man faithfully complied. He asked the bystanders to pray for him and said he would pray for them. He also asked that they pray for the king, that he would receive good counsel, and then said, "I die the king's servant, but God's first."

More knelt before the wooden block placed in the center of the scaffold and uttered his final audible prayer, the first line of Psalm 51: "Have mercy on me, O God, according to your steadfast love." Edward Hall, Undersheriff of London, later wrote that More bid the headsman, "Allow me to adjust my beard that it may not be cut, for it was never accused of treason."

~

The last lines of Sir Thomas More's hero story were written as his throat lay across the scarred and discolored surface of the wood, evidence of its previous use having been one of More's last earthly impressions. Accused of treason, he was in truth a man faithful to God and lawful authority dying a martyr's death for his religious convictions, freedom of conscience, and personal integrity. His seal in life had always been his word and his reputation for incorruptibility, and now in death his seal would be his blood. Hero stories of the saints often end in tragedy, and the lives of hero-saints are sometimes steeped in tragedy, yet it is through tragedy, both small and great, that hero-saints are made. For God uses tragedy to sanctify and purify his faithful servants and bring their virtue to perfection, and arrogant and inflexible men like those in this story sometimes meet their match in men like Thomas More, whose will they could not bend or break, nor his sanctity defile.

The head of Sir Thomas More did indeed roll, but King Henry would get no castle in France for it.

19

To the Last Tudor (1536 to 1603)

Catherine of Aragon died at Kimbolton Castle in the cold, damp fens of East Anglia on January 7, 1536, but her passing did not relieve the king of his widespread unpopularity. Henry and Anne celebrated by attending Mass and then dined with the court, but the merriness of the occasion (if it was at all genuine) would soon be replaced by fresh hardships and misfortune. On January 24, 1536, Henry fell from his horse while jousting at Greenwich and was knocked unconscious for two hours. The forty-four-year-old king sustained injuries that would remain with him for the rest of his life, and it was said that the mishap changed his personality. Three days later, and on the same day Catherine was buried at Peterborough, Anne miscarried. The unsympathetic king had her arrested on May 2 for alleged treason and several other trumped-up charges, including incest and adultery. She was imprisoned in the Tower and executed on May 19 along with her brother, Lord Rochford, and a few other courtiers. Henry granted her the final courtesy of hiring an expert swordsman from Calais who dispatched her with one stroke. (Multiple blows, sometimes four or five, were usually required if an axe were used.)

Henry's eyes had wandered from Anne even before the fatal blow had been struck and fell upon Jane Seymour, a modest and even-tempered young woman from Wiltshire with no aspiration for the queenship. She resisted his wooing, but the king could not accept a rebuff, and they were wed on May 30, 1536. Catherine's daughter, Mary Tudor, had already been declared illegitimate in the first Act of Succession of 1534, but Henry had a second Act of Succession passed in 1536 that declared both Mary and Anne's daughter, Elizabeth, illegitimate, and conferred succession on Henry's offspring with Jane. That same year, Henry's spirits were dampened further when his illegitimate son, Henry FitzRoy (1519–1536), Duke of Richmond and Somerset, who was born to his mistress Elizabeth Blount, died suddenly on July 23.

From 1536 to 1541, Henry suppressed all of the monasteries and religious houses in England under Cromwell's guidance and confiscated their lands and wealth. The Dissolution of the Monasteries replenished Henry's depleted coffers, and many of the properties were sold or leased to aristocratic families or courtiers. Jane finally provided Henry with his long-desired male heir when she gave birth to Edward VI on October 12, 1537, at Hampton Court Palace, but the gift would come at the cost of her life. She died twelve days later from complications of childbirth.

A fragile peace was concluded between France and the Holy Roman Empire on June 18, 1538, when the archrivals Francis I and Charles V signed the Treaty of Nice. England was left out of the agreement, and Henry found himself further isolated when Pope Paul III excommunicated him on December 17. Cromwell decided that the best policy would be for Henry to marry a foreign princess and secure a European alliance. Among the suitable candidates was Anne of Cleves (1515–1557), whom Henry selected based on a recent portrait of her and Cromwell's description. The king was sorely disappointed, however, when he found upon her arrival in England that she was much less attractive than she appeared in the painting. Henry could not afford to offend her German allies, so he married her but never consummated the marriage, and Anne received a generous settlement six months later in return for a divorce. Henry was again unforgiving, and Cromwell was arrested on June 10, 1540, for treason and heresy and executed on Tower Hill on July 28. The king soon regretted the deed, however, as Cromwell was a gifted minister and a man Henry could not easily replace.

Henry then married Catherine Howard (1523–1542) in July 1540, but the short-lived marriage ended on Tower Hill when the young, indiscreet woman (she was having an affair) was convicted of adultery and treason and beheaded on February 13, 1542. Catherine Parr (1512–1548), married twice previously, succeeded Howard in July 1543 as Henry's sixth and final wife. Her age and experience in marriage must have been of some benefit, for she conducted herself with prudence and kindness. Catherine was a good influence on Henry and brought stability to court life. She was kind to both of his daughters, Mary and Elizabeth, seeing to their well-being at court, and she was instrumental in having the third Act of Succession passed in 1544 which restored them to the line of succession. Catherine would be rewarded for her benevolence by outliving the king by more than a year.

~

And so came to an end the thirty-eight-year reign of King Henry VIII of England at about two o'clock in the morning on January 28, 1547. The news was kept secret for three days until Parliament was informed on January 31, 1547. According to his wishes, Henry was buried next to Jane Seymour, the mother of his heir, Edward VI (1537–1553).

Since Edward VI (r. 1547–1553) was only a boy at the time of his accession, the Regency Council appointed Edward Seymour as Lord Protector of the Realm and Governor of the King's Person. Seymour was the king's uncle and the older brother of Jane Seymour and was created Duke of Somerset early in Edward's reign. He was executed for treason in 1552, however, and his royal nephew died soon after of natural causes, which enabled Mary Tudor to ascend the throne. During Edward's reign, the government embraced Protestantism, but Mary I (r. 1553–1558) was a faithful Catholic, and she and her advisors attempted to restore Catholicism in England. This could not be done without much violence, however, and despite having executed almost three hundred persons,[30] she was unable to reverse the measures taken by her father and the government of her half-brother. Her decision to marry Philip II, King of Spain (1527–1598), was highly unpopular in England, and she died childless in 1558.

Next in the line of succession was Henry's third and final legitimate heir, Elizabeth I (r. 1558–1603), who embarked upon a long and successful reign that is credited with being one of the most glorious and stable in English history. She and her chief minister, Sir William Cecil (1520–1598)—who had served Edward VI and Mary I—engineered the Elizabethan Religious Settlement between Catholics and Protestants which prevented England from descending into the religious conflict that was plaguing the continent.

Elizabeth I, known among her subjects as "Good Queen Bess," died a popular queen in 1603, but she never married and so did not produce an heir. The Tudor dynasty came to an end with her passing, and James VI (1566–1625), King of Scotland, ascended the throne of England. Crowned James I, King of England (r. 1603–1625), he was a descendant of Henry VII and the first of the Stuart kings. England, Wales, and Scotland were now politically united for the first time under one king.

The political and religious turmoil experienced during the reigns of Henry VIII through Mary I was allayed somewhat during the reigns of Elizabeth I and James I, but this tranquility came at

---

[30] And in so doing earned the sobriquet "Bloody Mary."

a cost: Elizabeth declared Anglicanism the official religion of England and banned the outward observance of Catholicism in the Act of Uniformity of 1559. This legislation represented the almost complete defeat of Thomas More's objectives, and the faith he had died for in 1535 became illegal in England less than a quarter century later.

Yet the final word in his story was yet to be written.

Conclusion

This is a good point in the progress of this series to discuss two important and interrelated themes regarding hero-sainthood that are demonstrated vividly in the hero stories of Saint Joan of Arc (Book Two) and Saint Thomas More (Book Three): (1) Deus ex machina, and (2) reversal of fortune. We may view these themes and find evidence of them strictly in the historical record (a nonreligious approach), or we may add to this method the intent to view Joan and Thomas' stories (and all hero-saint stories) through the eyes of Christian faith. This second approach recognizes that even nonbelievers allow for the occurrence of Deus ex machina interventions (or moments) in a literary, if not religious, context.

Yet a strictly nonreligious approach is obviously not the object of this series, and the theology of hero-sainthood being developed in these books maintains that Deus ex machina (interventions or moments) and reversals of fortune may be experienced in this life, but only partially so, since the fullness of these realities can only be experienced in eternity. When viewed with the eyes of faith, the Deus ex machina and reversals of fortune that God worked in the lives of Joan and Thomas, for example, occurred primarily after their deaths. They went from being unjustly condemned and publicly executed as criminals to enjoying glorious reputations in history and eternity (as hero-figures and canonized saints). Conversely, evidence in the historical record suggests that those who persecuted Thomas and Joan did not fare well after their martyrdoms, and in any case, men like Pierre Cauchon, Nicolas Midy, Henry VIII, and Thomas Cranmer are simply not viewed in the same favorable light as Joan of Arc and Thomas More (and we certainly do not write hero stories about them!). There is an element of divine irony here.

Other important characteristics regarding these two themes are, first, that they are commonly, though not necessarily, found in the lives of other hero-saints, and they will appear again in the stories of Jesus of Nazareth and Maximilian Kolbe (but not in the fiction tale of Book Six). Second, reversals of fortune and Deus ex machina ordinarily take time to develop and require patience. Both Joan and Thomas were recognized among some of their contemporaries for their virtue and saintly heroism, but neither was canonized until the twentieth century. Third, these two themes apply not only to the earthly life of a hero-saint but also extend into the future events of history and eternity which can be far removed from the circumstances of their lives. In Joan's case, the Hundred Years' War did not end until twenty-two years after her death, even if her actions had much to do with its outcome. And as the dominoes of history fell, all of this had something to do with precipitating the Wars of the Roses—at least that is the view I took in this book.

In Thomas More's case (and to resume where the final chapter of this book ended), the Catholic liturgy and other Catholic practices remained illegal in England from the Act of Uniformity of 1559 until passage of the Catholic Emancipation Act in 1829 which restored the right of Catholics to hold public office and become members of Parliament. In 1850, Pope Pius IX published the bull *Universalis Ecclesiae* which reinstituted the Catholic hierarchy in England and then created Nicholas Wiseman (1802–1865) the Cardinal Archbishop of Westminster. Wiseman almost immediately began the canonization process of Thomas More and John Fisher, and both were beatified by Pope Leo XIII on the Feast of Saint Thomas Becket, December 29, 1886. This process was completed when they were canonized as martyrs by Pope Pius XI on May 19, 1935—the fourth centennial of their deaths—and More was named the Patron Saint of Lawyers. On October 31 of the Jubilee Year 2000, John Paul II named Thomas More the Patron Saint of Statesmen and Politicians. More and Fisher share the same feast day in the Roman Catholic calendar of saints (June 22), and in a remarkable turn of events that highlights the themes of Deus ex machina and reversal of fortune, the current calendar of the Church of England (since 2000) commemorates More and Fisher on July 6 as "Reformation Martyrs."

~

G. K. Chesterton spoke these prophetic words in 1929 in an address given at Chelsea:

> Thomas More is more important at this moment than at any moment since his death … but he is not quite so important as he will be in a hundred years' time.

May it please God that this little book, despite its inadequacies, might play some small role in the fulfillment of Chesterton's prophecy.

Afterword

Those who are familiar with the life of Thomas More or the history of the Reformation may be disappointed by the omission of so many important historical and biographical details in this account. There is much that could have been included but was not even mentioned (a criticism that applies to all of the historical books in this series). My approach is partly intentional, and while there is no shortage of histories and biographies in the world, I have not found much literature that is quite like hero stories, or studies in hero-sainthood, which is the real substance of my project.

My primary endeavor in this series is to develop a theology of hero-sainthood that begins with the concepts and themes in the "Lexicon of Terms" and the reflection "A Hero is Chosen" in Book One. For as enjoyable and profitable as history and biography are, the hero stories in this series are primarily intended to serve as *literary examples* or *case studies* of a few chosen souls who lived according to the Christian principles found in this theology of hero-sainthood—even if they were not consciously aware of them. Hero stories of the saints are *portraits* or *sketches* of persons who practiced heroic charity and made their earthly pilgrimage in the light of eternity—in a word, they are *literary illustrations* of hero-sainthood.

This series is a work in progress, and I am learning as I read, study, pray, reflect, and write. If many important historical and biographical details are absent from these accounts, then many important spiritual elements are surely missing as well. I simply have not figured it all out yet. But I know we need not identify *all* of the spiritual principles and understand *all* of the details of our personal mission and vocation to walk a path of hero-sainthood (did Joan, Thomas, Jesus, or Maximilian?). What is essential is *faith*. For God is ultimately in control, and we must let God be God. He alone has the power and wisdom to make us into the masterpiece of holiness he intends us to be. Knowledge of theology and the spiritual life is always helpful, but there is more to a life of holiness and hero-sainthood than can be found in the books in this series and all of the books in the whole world.

I suppose the same could be said of history.

About the Author

Brother Emmanuel Labrise, O.S.B., received a B.S. from Saint Vincent College, an M.A. from Bowling Green State University, and an M.A. from Notre Dame Seminary. A contemplative monk with over twenty years' experience in monastic life, he spent six years as a member of the Order of Carthusians and has been a monk in the Order of Saint Benedict since 2009. Among other assignments, he has taught in a seminary college, worked in a seminary formation program, and given conferences at a retreat house. He is currently living the eremitical life in which his main activities are prayer, reading, reflection, and writing.

Books by Brother Emmanuel Labrise, O.S.B.
A Hero Is Chosen Series
Hero Stories of the Saints

Book One: *Reflections of an Uncommon Monk: Toward a Theology of Hero-Sainthood*
Serves as an introduction to the series and its spiritual and moral foundation

Book Two: *Mission of the Maiden: The Hero Story of Joan of Arc*

    Part One: Historical Context
Fourteenth- and fifteenth-century medieval Europe; High Middle Ages; Hundred Years' War; history of France and England

    Part Two: Mission of the Maiden
Joan's hero-saint story focusing on her public mission (hero-event) from the time she left Domrémy until her interrogation, trial, and burning at the stake (hero-moment)

Book Three: *God's Good Servant and the King's: The Hero Story of Thomas More*

    Part One: Historical Context
Fifteenth- and sixteenth-century Renaissance Europe; Reformation period; English and Church history

    Part Two: God's Good Servant and the King's
Thomas More's hero-saint story focusing on his public dissent from King Henry VIII (hero-event) until his execution (hero-moment)

Notes and Personal Reflections: